The Silent Vault

The Silent Vault

Asset protection strategies from inflation, seizures, or collapse

Adrian Vossari

Mindful Pages

Published in 2025

ISBN: 9789371341783 (PB)
ISBN: 9789371341134 (eBook)

Published by

Mindful Pages
Imprint of Alpha Editions LLC
312 W. 2nd St #1834
Casper, WY 82601, USA

Content

Introduction
What If Everything You Own Isn't Really Yours?

There's a quiet deception woven through the fabric of modern life—one we rarely question. We're taught to believe that what's registered in our name belongs to us. The balance in your savings account, the equity in your home, the assets in your pension fund or brokerage account—even the digital tokens safely tucked into an online wallet. It all feels secure. But under closer examination, this sense of ownership begins to fray. What we now call "ownership" is less absolute than assumed. In truth, it is conditional—and, more troubling still, contingent.

Contingent upon the integrity of governments. The solvency of intermediaries. The smooth function of a vast, fragile digital infrastructure. The continuity of social contracts we neither drafted nor control. The truth is stark: your assets, your wealth—even your right to act—exist only insofar as the surrounding machinery continues to cooperate. If that cooperation breaks down? Many will find that what they thought they owned, they merely held—temporarily, and at the discretion of forces beyond their reach.

This book is written for those who feel a quiet unease. Not always spoken aloud, but persistent. A sense that the accepted mechanisms of ownership—the very structures once regarded as stable and sacrosanct—are now increasingly brittle, misaligned, or quietly extractive. It's for the investor who's watched deposit protections crumble, for the retiree seeing guarantees dissolve in real terms, for the founder who's had their funds frozen by faceless compliance. And equally, it's for the thinker, the realist, the cautious optimist—those who suspect that the concept of financial freedom has shifted from a right to a precarious allowance, one that can be withdrawn with alarming ease.

The Premise: Wealth is Conditional

We live in an age of dependencies so subtle they're almost invisible. A person can devote a lifetime to building wealth, only to find that they never truly possessed it. A sovereign default. A regulatory shift. A software error. An account locked—not through theft or violence, but by a line in a user agreement no one ever read. Legally sound. Institutionally sanctioned. And utterly destabilising. What remains, after such moments, is not ownership—it's exposure.

This book begins by pulling back that curtain. Not to frighten, but to reveal. To show that wealth in the modern age is buffered not by solid ground, but by a lattice of intermediaries—custodians, registries, courts, and code. While these systems are efficient when calm prevails, they become brittle under stress. Worse, they morph into tools of restriction, even coercion, in the hands of faltering institutions.

This is not conjecture. History supplies the evidence, time and again. When stress bears down, institutions serve their own survival first. From Cyprus to Argentina, from Weimar to 2008, the pattern repeats: access disappears first. Justified, sanctioned, irreversible. By the time the warning signs are clear, the gates have already closed. If you haven't prepared before that moment, preparation is no longer an option.

Not Just Protection—Transformation

The Silent Vault isn't simply a manual on shielding your assets. It's a prompt to reimagine the concept of wealth itself. This is not about evasion or fear. It's about agency. True wealth, in this frame, is not a static figure on a quarterly statement. It's a composite of capabilities—discretion, portability, resilience, and sovereignty. Risk can't be eliminated, and this book won't pretend otherwise. But your assets can be made harder to detect, more difficult to confiscate, and less susceptible to systemic fragility.

You'll not find in these pages the standard fare of financial advice. No portfolio rebalancing templates or trendy asset classes. What you will find is something deeper: a cross-disciplinary weave of historical precedent, psychological insight, legal nuance, technological tools, and real-world strategy. Asset protection here is not a checklist. It's a philosophical posture—a quiet insistence that the future must be self-authored, not dictated.

Strategy Meets Sovereignty

Each chapter is designed not merely to inform, but to challenge. To question what you think you know about safety, access, and control. Chapter 1, *The Illusion of Ownership*, explores the infrastructure that props up the very notion of property. It reveals how possession depends less on what you hold and more on whether the systems agree you hold it—and what happens when that agreement falters.

Chapter 2, *The Psychology of Seizure*, probes our emotional susceptibility to control. Why do we tolerate creeping overreach? Why do we normalise it? The chapter unpacks the subtle psychological patterns—trauma loops, safety myths, bias towards institutional trust—that keep us docile even as our autonomy erodes. Understanding these instincts isn't just empowering—it's a defence.

Chapter 3 pivots to history. In *A History of Hidden Wealth*, we examine how individuals and families have safeguarded their capital under duress. These are not tales of paranoia, but blueprints of resilience. Gold sealed in false walls. Ledgers written in cipher. Grey economies humming beneath collapsing states. The actors change; the pattern endures.

Chapters 4 and 5 mark the shift into architecture. *Redefining Wealth in a Collapsing World* teaches you to revalue your assets through the lenses of liquidity, privacy, and systemic independence. What you can move. What you can shield. What you can rely on when the formal scaffolding buckles. Then, in *Currencies of the Future (and Past)*, we explore the changing terrain of value itself—Bitcoin, barter, metals, social credit, and the age-old logic of tangible, borderless mediums in an increasingly watched world.

From here, theory gives way to structure. Chapters 6 and 7—*Hiding in Plain Sight* and *The Sovereign Portfolio*—introduce the techniques and frameworks for building a stealth-resilient posture. Think jurisdictional arbitrage, decentralised systems, portable income. These tools don't hide your wealth out of fear. They allow it to breathe, flex, and adapt without permission.

Chapter 8, *Beyond Borders, Beyond Banking*, reconsiders geography not as a constraint, but as a design variable. Stateless residency, virtual domiciles, identity arbitrage—this isn't escapism. It's about future-proofing. Mobility, once a luxury, is now a strategic requirement.

But structure without soul is empty. Chapter 9, *The Ethics of Escape*, asks the hard questions. Is financial independence inherently selfish in a world of inequality? Where does self-preservation become abandonment? What do we owe to the systems that no longer protect us? This isn't a detour. It's the core of the conversation. Any strategy worth its salt must also answer to conscience.

Finally, *Exercises in Sovereignty* grounds the entire journey in tangible action. From risk audits to scenario drills, from threat modelling to escape planning—this chapter closes the loop. You'll emerge with a blueprint, not just a book.

The Real Vault is Silent

Why the name *The Silent Vault*? Because true protection isn't declared. It doesn't wave flags or wear labels. It's unassuming. Quiet. Strategic. A silent vault is not illegal—it simply doesn't register in the usual databases. It lives in unmonitored networks, embodied knowledge, and robust yet untraceable design. It isn't a fantasy. It's already here, quietly built by those who sense that tomorrow's security won't be granted—it must be created.

A Timeless Urgency

The threats catalogued here—confiscation, inflation, systemic failure—are not modern inventions. They are ancient, recurring. What's new is the speed, reach, and surveillance capacity with which they now occur. But with that comes a counterweight: unprecedented tools for self-defence, if one knows how to wield them.

This is not a call for isolationism or cynicism. It is an invitation to deliberate design. To step beyond reaction into intention. To prepare, not because disaster is inevitable, but because resilience is prudent.

The moment to act is not after the headlines arrive. It is before. While you still have the freedom to choose. By the end of this book, you'll have more than ideas. You'll have a framework—and perhaps, just as critically, a clearer sense of where not to place your trust.

Let us begin.

Chapter 1
The Illusion of Ownership

What does it mean to *own* something in this century—not in the legalistic sense, nor with the sentimentality of heirlooms, but in the concrete, no-one-can-take-it-from-you sense of control? It's a question so fundamental that it tends to go unasked. Most people, when they glance at their savings, survey their property, or check their investment portfolios, assume an unspoken certainty: that what's theirs is, in fact, theirs. That they hold ultimate authority over it. Yet this assumption, so casual and widespread, may be one of the most hazardous illusions of our age.

In reality, ownership has been quietly redefined. It is no longer absolute—it's conditional. Conditional not merely upon economic tides or political continuity, but upon a matrix of custodial layers that have, over time, become so commonplace they are nearly invisible. Gatekeepers are embedded in nearly every transaction, every record, every right. This is not a conspiratorial notion. It's the design.

Examine your own financial landscape, and the pattern reveals itself. The very tools created to protect your wealth often carry the built-in authority to restrict your access to it. Your bank? It's not just holding your money—it decides when and how you get to use it. Your brokerage account? It may show your name, but the legal ownership often sits with a third-party custodian. Even your home, legally "yours," is but a record in a government ledger—subject to change, error, or interference. And with a few lines of code or a policy shift, that "ownership" can be questioned, suspended, or erased. In effect, modern ownership is not control—it's permission.

Even the language we use is telling. We "deposit" money into banks that require us to "request" withdrawals. We "own" stock held by intermediaries we've never met, whose solvency we must simply trust. Cryptocurrencies, once the poster child of decentralised autonomy, have been repackaged into custodial platforms that mimic the very institutions they sought to circumvent. The harsh truth? If you don't control the keys, you don't control the asset. And if someone else can delay, deny, or determine your access, then what you possess isn't property—it's a provisional claim.

This chapter aims to peel back the comfort of that illusion—not with melodrama, but with sober scrutiny. The issue at hand isn't necessarily malice, but architecture. What we accept as ownership today is a construct mediated by systems designed to operate smoothly—until they don't. And when they falter, as all systems eventually do, it becomes clear that the corridor we mistook for a vault is, in fact, lined with switches that we didn't install and cannot flip.

It is one of the cruel ironies of the digital era: as access to capital and information has grown exponentially, the means of control have tightened. Yes, you can move funds faster than ever—but the surveillance surrounding those transactions is equally swift. Yes, your wealth is now portable—but it's also traceable, taxable, and, increasingly, interruptible. The grand narrative of personal financial freedom, sold to us alongside touchless payments and intuitive dashboards, conceals a more sobering reality: the more digitised your assets, the more easily they can be locked, altered, or deleted—by actors you may never meet, for reasons you may never be told.

This brings us to the figure of the custodian—a term that sounds benign, even protective. But custodianship in financial systems is a power dynamic, not a service. Consider Cyprus in 2013. One morning, bank account holders awoke to discover a portion of their deposits had been seized—excused later as a "bail-in." Or Canada, 2022, when government orders froze the bank accounts of protestors—not through trial or due process, but through executive fiat. Or the growing number of cases where platforms like PayPal or Stripe have suspended user accounts without notice, often citing opaque policy breaches with no clear recourse. These aren't historical footnotes. They're precedents.

And they're becoming less exceptional. The logic underpinning modern financial systems has shifted—from one of assumed permission to one of conditional access. You may operate freely, until flagged. You may retain your funds, unless questioned. It's a subtle recalibration, but its effects are sweeping: the presumption of ownership has been replaced by the presumption of compliance.

Digitisation has accelerated this shift. Where once records were physical—held in local offices, checked by hand, governed by locality—they are now lines in global databases, vulnerable to cyberattacks, policy pivots, or mere software glitches. Your assets can be frozen by algorithm. Your transactions flagged by AI. A revised terms-of-service clause, quietly published, may alter your access without your knowledge. The process is bloodless, paperless, and often irreversible. And nearly all of it unfolds behind interfaces designed to feel seamless, friendly—trustworthy.

What complicates this further is the emotional scaffolding of modern finance. Its systems don't just function through code and policy—they operate through your own psychology. They're built to exploit fear: fear of noncompliance, of suspicion, of the reputational cost of questioning the rules. But perhaps more powerfully, they exploit your fear of stepping outside. To withdraw—to deal in cash, to use self-custodied crypto, to trade directly—is to step into a domain where *you* must defend your legitimacy. You become the anomaly. The deviant. The one who must prove innocence rather than presume it.

This is no accident. Fear is not an unintended consequence—it's the lubricant that keeps the machinery compliant. Financial infrastructure encourages dependency through inertia. Think of your direct debits, auto-payments, rewards points, credit history. All of it engineered to reward staying in-system and to punish divergence. The deeper your integration, the harder the exit becomes. And should the machinery begin to falter—as it has, and as it will—the costs of leaving may already be intolerable.

So we arrive at a contradiction, almost poetic in its irony. Never before has human civilisation generated so much wealth, so quickly—and never has the claim to that wealth been more fragile. Modern ownership is a kind of theatre. Keep to the script, stay within the lines, and you're free to act as if what you have is secure. But stray outside the accepted frame—geographically, politically, philosophically—and the stagehands appear, ushering you offstage.

This chapter lays bare that stagecraft. It examines the legal frameworks, institutional logics, and digital mechanisms that conspire—often without intent—to hollow out the substance of ownership while preserving its appearance. It reveals how the tools meant to simplify and streamline our lives also encode new forms of vulnerability, and how the systems we assume to be neutral are, in fact, deeply invested in compliance.

This erosion is not restricted to authoritarian regimes or failing economies. It is happening, quietly and lawfully, in places that still call themselves free. The paperwork is tidy. The policies are published. The levers are pulled not with malice, but with indifference. And the result is the same: power without oversight, control without consent.

You will not find here a prescription for withdrawal into the wilderness. This isn't a call to renounce technology or reject civilisation. But it is an invitation to examine, honestly and without flinching, the infrastructure of control beneath the illusion of autonomy. Because the illusion will hold only as long as it remains unexamined.

What follows is not a manifesto. It is a reckoning. And eventually, a reorientation. This chapter will not soothe you—but it will, if you let it, sharpen your awareness. And that, perhaps, is the first real possession: clarity. The kind that can't be revoked.

The Paper Castle

Ownership is one of civilisation's most powerful constructs. It grants security, status, and freedom. It shapes identity and inheritance. To "own" something is to possess both the rights to it and the authority over it. Or so we are told. But peel back the polished exterior of modern ownership and you discover not a granite foundation, but a paper castle—an intricate façade of legal codes, institutional permissions, and bureaucratic consensus that can be altered, contested, or dissolved without your consent.

The concept of ownership today is not grounded in physical possession, nor in any universal truth. It is, in almost every case, a legal fiction. You do not own your home in any practical sense—you hold a title, recognised by a registry, enforced by courts, and subject to conditions defined by legislation that can shift without your input. You do not truly own your savings—they are entries in a bank's internal system, which owes you a liability denominated in a national currency that itself is subject to policy, inflation, and systemic failure. Even corporate shares, digital assets, or intellectual property depend on enforcement mechanisms and recognition from intermediaries who are, in the final analysis, more loyal to the state than to the individual.

What we take for granted as ownership is, in most cases, a claim acknowledged within a framework of laws, upheld by third parties, and protected only as long as the system agrees to protect it. When the system falters—through crisis, corruption, or coercion—the claim becomes a suggestion, and the fiction is exposed.

Take, for example, the 2008 financial crisis. Millions of people discovered that the deeds to their homes did not protect them from mass foreclosure. Robo-signing scandals revealed that major institutions had been fabricating legal documents to push through evictions at scale. Property rights, supposedly sacrosanct, were collateral damage in a system prioritising balance sheets over justice. In theory, a homeowner with a clean mortgage record should have been invulnerable. In practice, legal ownership was only as strong as the integrity of the institutions backing it.

This is not confined to the United States. In Greece, during the sovereign debt crisis, property taxes were suddenly tied to electricity bills—if you refused to pay, your power was cut off. The message was unambiguous: your right to your property is subject to your compliance. More recently, in places like Turkey and India, shifts in political will have led to abrupt changes in land use laws and retroactive zoning restrictions, effectively eroding ownership rights overnight. These are not isolated incidents—they are symptoms of a deeper truth: ownership, when mediated by paper and policy, is only stable until it's not.

To understand how this fragility is constructed, we must look at the architecture of modern asset recognition. At the centre is the registry—a government-managed or institutionally governed database that records who owns what. This might be a land registry, a shareholder register, a patent office, or a centralised ledger in a bank or exchange. These registries are, in effect, the definitive source of truth. If your name appears there, you're entitled. If it doesn't, you are not. And yet these systems, however authoritative they seem, are deeply fallible.

They can be hacked, altered, or mismanaged. In 2016, a major cyberattack on the Bangladesh Central Bank exploited SWIFT messaging systems to reroute $81 million in a matter of hours. The money moved not through violence or fraud in the traditional sense, but through the manipulation of digital records—paper, upgraded to code, and still no less brittle. In developing countries, land registry records are routinely disputed or corrupted, either by accident or by design. In fact, the World Bank estimates that over 70% of land in emerging economies lacks formal legal title. That is not an absence of property—it is an absence of recognised paperwork. The ownership still exists in the minds and customs of communities. But in the paper-based system of global finance and law, that ownership is invisible.

Even in countries with robust legal frameworks, the enforceability of ownership depends on courts—institutions that are slow, expensive, and often biased towards entrenched power. Possession might be nine-tenths of the law, but the remaining tenth—the legal recognition—is where real authority lies. And it is precisely there that most individuals have the least control.

This gap between possession and recognition is further widened by financial intermediaries. When you "own" stocks, what you actually hold is a contractual claim on a brokerage, which itself holds the shares in street name through a clearinghouse. Your name does not appear on the corporate share register. If the broker collapses or the clearinghouse is compromised, your asset may become entangled in litigation, frozen, or simply inaccessible. The 2021 GameStop episode highlighted this fragility. Trading platforms like Robinhood restricted users from buying shares—not because of any market rule, but because of liquidity pressures from their own clearing partners. The ability to transact was revoked, not by law, but by internal policy—a striking reminder that access to your assets can be curtailed without your consent and often without warning.

Digital assets, despite their promise of decentralisation, are not exempt. Most cryptocurrency holders store their tokens on centralised exchanges. These platforms, as recent scandals like the FTX collapse have shown, are not decentralised banks but lightly regulated custodians. When FTX went under, billions in customer funds vanished. Users who thought they held digital assets discovered they merely had IOUs. Once again, the paper—this time in the form of digital dashboards—was meaningless without the underlying control.

This fragility is compounded by the layered dependency on contracts—those dense, unread documents filled with clauses, contingencies, and escape hatches. Contracts are not instruments of equality; they are mechanisms of power. Their enforceability depends on your resources, your jurisdiction, and your leverage. A corporation with a legal team will always be in a stronger position than an individual trying to enforce a service agreement or recover a disputed asset. And when enforcement itself is outsourced to arbitration panels or regulatory bodies, the idea of fair ownership becomes even murkier.

Philosophically, this raises a profound question: if your ownership is only recognised when intermediaries say so, and only protected when systems function, then what do you actually own? The Stoics argued that only what is under your direct control can be considered truly yours. Everything else is subject to external interference. In this sense, modern ownership is more illusion than asset—more promise than power.

Yet the systems that maintain this illusion are not accidental. They are meticulously designed to optimise efficiency, scalability, and—most importantly—compliance. A centralised registry is easier to tax, monitor, and seize. A digital record is easier to modify. A legal framework is easier to reinterpret. And when ownership exists only within this framework, the state or institution that governs it holds the ultimate veto. It can nationalise, confiscate, legislate, or simply delay, all under the colour of law.

This is not to argue for abandoning the idea of legal ownership altogether, but to confront its limitations honestly. The paper castle is not inherently malicious—it's just structurally weak. And when built on shifting sands of policy, regulation, and technological centralisation, it becomes a risk to those who assume its permanence.

So what are the implications for those seeking to protect their wealth—not just in theory, but in practice? First, it requires a shift in mindset. Ownership must be understood not as a binary state, but as a spectrum of control. The closer your asset is to your physical reach or your cryptographic key, the more secure your ownership. The further it lies in the hands of institutions, systems, or laws, the more vulnerable it becomes.

Second, diversification must be redefined—not just across asset classes, but across custodial models. It is not enough to hold stocks, property, and crypto. One must ask: *Who holds them for me? Where are they registered? What jurisdiction governs them?* These are not peripheral details—they are the architecture of your control.

Third, legal resilience must be designed into your holdings. That means understanding the terms and conditions of every contract, account, and title. It means exploring structures like offshore trusts, private vaults, or self-custodied digital wallets—not to evade responsibility, but to decentralise risk.

Finally, we must accept that ownership in the traditional sense is no longer a guarantee. It is a claim that must be defended—legally, technically, and psychologically. And defending it starts with recognising the paper for what it is: a symbol, not a shield.

The paper castle stands tall in the modern mind because we want it to. It represents order, legitimacy, and a promise that the system will hold. But promises are not guarantees, and appearances are not protection. Real ownership today begins where the paperwork ends—with knowledge, preparation, and the willingness to step outside the illusion.

Custodians or Captors?

We are conditioned to believe that the institutions safeguarding our wealth operate as neutral stewards—reliable, trustworthy, and fundamentally aligned with our interests. Banks are where we "keep" our money. Brokers "hold" our investments. Governments "guarantee" our deposits. These third parties are cast in the role of custodians: facilitators of access, protectors of value, providers of infrastructure. And for the majority of people, most of the time, this illusion is never disturbed.

But custodianship, as structured in modern finance, is not neutral. It is not passive. It is not even, strictly speaking, custodial. It is a position of conditional control—one in which the intermediary, not the owner, retains ultimate authority over when, how, and whether assets can be accessed, transferred, or liquidated. And once this asymmetry is acknowledged, the roles shift. Custodians reveal themselves not just as facilitators, but as potential captors.

The power held by financial intermediaries is rarely questioned because it is exercised subtly. Most control is not applied through overt expropriation, but through defaults, permissions, and friction.

If your bank account is frozen, your broker halts trading, or your payment processor suspends services, you have few immediate remedies. You may own the asset on paper, but you do not possess the means to act upon that ownership without permission. That is not true control—it is conditional access.

This conditionality is not a design flaw; it is a feature. It enables regulatory compliance, policy enforcement, and, in crisis scenarios, systemic preservation. But it also means that during periods of political instability, financial turbulence, or regulatory overreach, intermediaries can pivot from protector to gatekeeper with extraordinary speed—and often without warning.

Consider the 2022 freezing of bank accounts in Canada, a liberal democracy with strong rule-of-law traditions. In response to the "Freedom Convoy" protests, the federal government invoked emergency powers, directing financial institutions to freeze personal and corporate accounts linked to protest activity. No court order was necessary. No criminal charges were required. The presumption of innocence was irrelevant. Major banks complied swiftly and silently. For many Canadians, the event shattered the implicit trust that banks would remain apolitical custodians of capital. The institutions acted not as neutral actors, but as extensions of state enforcement.

To frame this as an anomaly is to misunderstand the structure of modern financial governance. Banks are not designed to act independently of government interest; they are deeply enmeshed in the regulatory apparatus. They depend on charters, licences, insurance schemes, and access to central bank liquidity. Their survival is linked to their compliance. This makes them remarkably efficient as instruments of state policy—not just in times of war or emergency, but also in the quiet everyday enforcement of financial norms. The same applies to payment processors, fintech companies, and brokerage platforms. Each one functions within a compliance ecosystem that prioritises surveillance, reporting, and sanction enforcement above customer sovereignty.

This convergence between custodianship and control is particularly stark in global financial networks. Cross-border payments, offshore holdings, and multi-currency accounts are not immune; they are often *more* vulnerable. The SWIFT network, which facilitates most international interbank transfers, is based in Belgium but effectively controlled by US financial regulations. When geopolitical sanctions are imposed, access to SWIFT becomes a tool of economic warfare. Iran, Russia, and Venezuela have all experienced full or partial exclusion, crippling their ability to trade globally. While these are sovereign states, not individuals, the principle holds: control over financial infrastructure equals control over access to capital. For private citizens with assets in foreign banks or accounts in regulated exchanges, the same levers exist—just more discreetly.

Brokers and custodial investment platforms operate on similar principles. When you buy equities or ETFs through a brokerage, you do not take possession of the underlying securities. Instead, you are issued a contractual claim. The brokerage retains actual custody, typically through a clearinghouse or central securities depository. This arrangement works smoothly until it doesn't. During periods of volatility or liquidity stress, brokers have been known to halt trading, limit withdrawals, or restrict certain asset classes entirely—without client consent.

The 2021 GameStop trading halt by Robinhood is a case in point. The brokerage, facing collateral requirements from clearinghouses, froze the ability of users to buy (but not sell) certain securities. While this was technically a liquidity management decision, the optics and outcome were clear: retail traders, believing themselves to have full agency, discovered that their access could be unilaterally curtailed. The question of ownership became secondary to the fact of dependency.

Dependency is the core issue. When your assets are held by someone else, your freedom to act is dependent on their solvency, their infrastructure, their terms of service, and their regulatory obligations.

That dependence is rarely visible during stable periods, but in moments of crisis, it asserts itself with brutal clarity.

During the 2008 financial crisis, clients of Lehman Brothers discovered this firsthand. The firm's bankruptcy left thousands of investors in legal limbo. Assets held in supposedly segregated accounts were tangled in litigation for years. Clients had assumed that segregation meant safety. In practice, it meant being last in line behind creditors, administrators, and legal fees. Even now, many investors do not realise that their "segregated" brokerage accounts may still be pooled at the clearing level—a technicality that can have catastrophic implications under stress.

This is not just a matter of technical structure—it is a matter of philosophical clarity. What does it mean to *own* something if someone else can decide when, how, and if you can use it? That question is no longer academic. With the rise of programmable money, central bank digital currencies (CBDCs), and algorithmic compliance systems, the distance between custodianship and control is shrinking even further. Future financial infrastructure may not just enable state oversight—it may automate it.

CBDCs, currently in development or pilot in dozens of countries, are often framed as innovations in efficiency. In reality, they represent a paradigm shift in control. With CBDCs, governments could hypothetically restrict purchases, apply expiry dates to funds, or freeze balances at the push of a button. These are not theoretical capabilities—they are design choices. And if implemented through the centralised architecture of state-linked intermediaries, they will transform custodianship into direct programmable constraint.

The implications are profound. The architecture of financial custody is shifting from a model of implied neutrality to one of conditional permission. This shift is not limited to authoritarian regimes or underdeveloped markets. It is playing out in liberal democracies, through law, technology, and institutional evolution.

To respond effectively, individuals must begin to distinguish between ownership and access, between possession and control. Holding assets in your name does not make them yours in practice. *If access is mediated, then control is externalised.* And external control is always a vector of vulnerability.

There are, of course, legitimate arguments in favour of custodial systems. They reduce fraud, enable recourse, support compliance, and allow for systemic integration. But these benefits must be weighed against the risks—particularly as the balance of power between individual and institution becomes increasingly asymmetric. For many, that balance has already tilted too far.

The way forward requires not panic, but precision. It is possible to build financial lives that incorporate the benefits of infrastructure without ceding all control. This means understanding the custody arrangements behind your assets. It means favouring non-custodial tools where possible. It means holding a portion of wealth in forms that are not reliant on counterparties—whether that's physical cash, allocated precious metals, or cryptographic assets under personal key control.

It also means political awareness. The question of financial custodianship is not just technical—it is civic. If we accept the merging of policy enforcement with personal finance without scrutiny, we normalise a future in which dissent becomes not illegal, but unaffordable.

None of this is to argue that custodianship is inherently malicious. But *unquestioned custodianship is inherently dangerous.* Whether your assets are held by a bank, a broker, or a state, the same principle applies: the power to protect is also the power to prevent. And in times of stress, the difference between the two is defined not by law, but by institutional interest.

The challenge, then, is to become literate in the structure of our own dependencies. Only when we understand how power is exercised over what we think we own can we begin to recover true financial agency. That may involve different choices for different people. But the first step is the same for all: stop mistaking custodianship for freedom.

The Fragility of the Grid

At the core of modern wealth lies a paradox. The very technologies that have made capital more fluid, accessible, and borderless have also rendered it uniquely fragile—exposed to risks that were unthinkable in a paper-bound world. Digitisation has not merely upgraded financial infrastructure; it has redefined the terms of ownership, custody, and control. What once resided in vaults, safes, and ledgers now exists largely as code—visible, transferable, and revocable at a speed and scale that would have astonished prior generations. And with this shift, a silent vulnerability has emerged: *if your wealth lives on the grid, then it lives at the mercy of the grid.*

The digital grid—comprising banking systems, cloud servers, authentication protocols, centralised registries, and telecommunications infrastructure—is both vast and invisible to the average user. We interact with it daily without understanding its architecture. Tap a phone to pay, refresh an account balance, authorise a transfer—all of it feels seamless. But this seamlessness is deceptive. It conceals a growing dependence on an infrastructure that is not only centralised and opaque, but increasingly brittle under pressure.

The fragility of this grid can be examined across three interlocking dimensions: *susceptibility to freezing*, *vulnerability to hacking*, and *potential for erasure*. Each represents a mode of failure that, while technically distinct, shares a common implication: when trust in the grid is compromised, access to wealth becomes uncertain. Not lost in the traditional sense—not stolen, burned, or devalued—but rendered temporarily or permanently inaccessible, with limited avenues for recourse.

1. Freezing: Control Disguised as Security

One of the least understood yet most potent features of digital wealth is how easily it can be frozen. In traditional systems, cutting off access to funds required legal process, physical intervention, or explicit court orders. Today, it often requires little more than an API call or an internal compliance flag.

Consider the infrastructure behind a typical bank account. The balance you see is not an isolated entity—it is a permissioned reflection of your standing within a centralised ledger maintained by a financial institution. That institution is embedded in a legal and regulatory ecosystem where it is required, or at times incentivised, to act upon various signals: suspicion of fraud, regulatory inquiry, geopolitical sanctions, or even mere association with flagged individuals or causes. Your funds may not be seized outright, but they can be *suspended*, pending investigation, clarification, or confirmation of identity. The mechanism for freezing is instant; the unfreezing is bureaucratic, slow, and often Kafkaesque.

The scope of freeze-based control has expanded dramatically in recent years. Payment processors—Stripe, PayPal, Square, among others—frequently lock accounts for "suspicious activity" that is never clearly defined. Cryptocurrency exchanges, although framed as decentralised finance platforms, regularly comply with regional regulations, freezing wallets or denying service based on jurisdictional mandates. Even crowdfunding platforms have joined this trend. In several high-profile cases, donations to politically sensitive causes were seized, rerouted, or returned—not based on illegality, but on reputational or compliance considerations. The implication is stark: digital infrastructure doesn't just move money; it *filters it.*

The notion that wealth can be frozen without trial, due process, or even a clear explanation speaks to a deep structural shift. Control no longer needs to be exercised through physical enforcement or legal process; it can be embedded in code and policy. And because freezing is often portrayed as a temporary measure, it avoids the legal scrutiny that outright confiscation might provoke. But temporary can become indefinite. And indefinite, in financial terms, is a euphemism for loss.

2. Hacking: The Myth of Digital Infallibility

While freezing stems from *intentional* control by institutions, hacking represents *unintentional* failure—a collapse not of policy, but of integrity. And as digitisation expands, so too does the attack surface of the financial grid.

In 2016, hackers stole approximately $81 million from the Bangladesh Central Bank by exploiting vulnerabilities in the SWIFT global messaging system. This wasn't the act of rogue insiders or petty criminals. It was a technically sophisticated operation that manipulated authentication systems and transaction flows—within a system trusted globally by thousands of institutions. The attack demonstrated that even the most guarded financial networks are susceptible to precision strikes.

More recently, high-profile breaches at cryptocurrency exchanges like Mt. Gox, Bitfinex, and Coincheck revealed just how porous digital custody can be. In each case, customers who believed their funds were secured in high-tech systems learned that technical sophistication is no substitute for resilience. Billions in value were erased in moments—not by market collapse, but by unauthorised access. The illusion of impenetrability was replaced by the reality of untraceability.

Cyberattacks do not only target institutions. Increasingly, individuals are vulnerable through phishing, SIM swaps, and compromised two-factor authentication protocols. The more tightly wealth is tied to a digital identity—email, device, biometric—the more exposed it becomes to sophisticated forms of identity theft. A compromised password can lead to emptied accounts. A stolen phone can grant access to wallets. Even a fake app, mimicking a legitimate exchange, can siphon off holdings without detection. The grid, once breached, offers little mercy.

What makes these risks especially perilous is that digital theft often lacks visibility. Unlike a stolen vehicle or physical intrusion, hacked assets can vanish silently. Detection may take hours or days; recovery, if possible, is slow and uncertain. Law enforcement, often unfamiliar with blockchain forensics or decentralised finance tools, offers little assurance. In the digital domain, speed favours the attacker.

3. Erasure: When the Ledger Fails

The third and most existential risk of digitised wealth is erasure—not theft, not denial, but disappearance. While this may sound extreme, it is a growing concern in an age of centralised data, platform dependency, and increasingly politicised technology policy.

At its core, digital wealth is information. Your ownership of a stock, bond, or token is merely a record on a server—a database entry that depends on electrical continuity, institutional cooperation, and data integrity. If that record is corrupted, deleted, or rolled back, your claim to ownership evaporates. This is not hypothetical. In 2012, Knight Capital, a major US trading firm, lost $440 million in 45 minutes due to a software error. The glitch led to thousands of erroneous trades—many of which were cancelled, while others were enforced—causing massive disruptions. Errors in code became errors in capital.

In less transparent systems, particularly in emerging markets, erasure can be systemic and deliberate. Government databases can be rewritten. Ownership records can be lost, tampered with, or retroactively adjusted. This is particularly evident in politically volatile regions where regime change often brings asset redistribution or land reallocation. In such environments, the "grid" is not a neutral system—it is a political weapon.

Even in mature democracies, the dependency on cloud-based systems and proprietary software introduces new risks. What happens if a platform fails, is taken offline, or is blocked at a national firewall level? How many individuals hold wealth in the form of game assets, subscription credits, or platform-specific tokens that could vanish with a terms-of-service update or corporate bankruptcy?

The question is no longer whether such erasure is likely—it is *when* and *where* it will occur next. And more critically, *what recourse* the individual will have. Often, the answer is none.

The Illusion of Permanence

The common thread through these vulnerabilities is the illusion of permanence. Digital wealth *feels* secure because it is omnipresent, updated in real time, and instantly retrievable. But that perception masks the extent to which access is conditional and continuity is fragile. The very features that make digital assets attractive—liquidity, speed, decentralisation—are often built on foundations that are brittle, opaque, or reversible.

This is not an argument against digitisation. The efficiency gains are real. But it is a warning against uncritical dependence. To mistake digital presence for resilience is to misread the nature of technological systems. *All digital systems are fallible; the only question is how they fail, and whether you can recover when they do.*

Resilience, then, is not built by avoiding the grid, but by understanding its weaknesses—and designing redundancies accordingly. That may mean holding a portion of assets offline, in cold wallets or physical form. It may involve structuring portfolios with jurisdictional diversity, decentralised custody, or legal insulation. Most importantly, it requires mental discipline: recognising that what is accessible is not always secure, and what is secure is not always accessible.

The fragility of the grid is not a reason to retreat into financial nostalgia or techno-paranoia. It is a call for clarity—for a sober, technically literate, and philosophically grounded understanding of what wealth really means in a world where its representation has become weightless, invisible, and instantly revocable.

To live in a digitised financial system is not optional. But how we participate in it—*how much trust we extend, how much exposure we tolerate, and how much redundancy we build*—is very much a choice. One that becomes more urgent with every update, outage, breach, or freeze.

Fear as a Feature

Most modern financial systems are not built to imprison overtly. They are not tyrannical in the traditional sense, nor do they rely on open coercion to enforce participation. Instead, they function by engineering inertia—by creating conditions in which opting out feels irrational, self-destructive, or outright terrifying. In such systems, fear is not an accident or unfortunate side effect; it is a design principle. *Fear is the cost of exit—and the glue of dependency.*

This fear does not announce itself with the blunt force of repression. It manifests through complexity, uncertainty, and the subtle but persistent threat of exclusion. To imagine walking away from the conventional grid—be it banking, healthcare, taxation, or mainstream employment—is to invite a long list of unanswerable questions. How will I access my funds? What happens to my credit score? Will I be able to rent a flat, get a loan, or prove my identity? These aren't trivial concerns—they are the scaffolding of modern life. And the deeper you are embedded, the more existential the threat of disconnection becomes.

This dynamic—where systems make exit psychologically or practically prohibitive—is neither accidental nor new. It has deep roots in political philosophy, behavioural economics, and institutional strategy. From Hobbes's Leviathan to Foucault's analysis of disciplinary societies, thinkers have long recognised that control is most effective not when it punishes defection, but when it makes defection feel unthinkable. What's different now is how this control operates through the infrastructure of daily life—through the interface of a banking app, a compliance form, or an algorithmically filtered service—and how thoroughly it is normalised.

To see this clearly, one must first understand the architecture of dependency. Financial systems today do not merely hold assets; they *mediate identity*. Your bank account is not just a place to store value—it is a proxy for your legitimacy. Without it, you are economically invisible. Consider how many aspects of modern life now require financial verification: signing a lease, registering for utilities, subscribing to essential services, even passing basic background checks. The system makes no overt threats, but the message is clear: *without us, you don't exist.*

This creates a form of *soft coercion*—what legal scholars sometimes call structural coercion. It doesn't deny you the right to leave, but it makes staying feel safer, more rational, even morally superior. In many countries, for instance, withdrawing significant cash from a bank raises red flags. You're free to do it, of course, but you'll be questioned, reported, possibly profiled. The act of reclaiming physical custody of your own money has become coded as suspicious. That coding is not legal in the traditional sense—it's psychological. It turns agency into anxiety.

Fear also flourishes in the language of regulation. Know Your Customer (KYC) and Anti-Money Laundering (AML) frameworks are, in principle, protections against fraud and crime. In practice, they create a labyrinth of documentation, surveillance, and compliance burdens that make financial self-direction feel hazardous. Want to open a foreign bank account? Expect to explain yourself, repeatedly, to people who owe you no accountability. Want to use privacy-enhancing financial tools? Prepare to be associated with criminality. The threat here isn't prosecution—it's reputational erosion and administrative obstruction.

Behavioural economics offers a lens into how this dependency is internalised. Daniel Kahneman's concept of *loss aversion*—our tendency to fear losses more than we value equivalent gains—explains why even the idea of leaving the system feels irrational to many. The perceived loss of convenience, credibility, or security outweighs the potential gain in sovereignty. This aversion is compounded by *status quo bias*, which makes the default option feel not only familiar, but right. Together, these biases render the system's grip largely self-enforcing. It doesn't have to chain you—it merely has to convince you that freedom is riskier than servitude.

We see this dynamic play out acutely in times of crisis, when systems use fear to reinforce dependency under the guise of protection. During the COVID-19 pandemic, for example, digital surveillance expanded dramatically. Health status apps, travel permits, and emergency financial disbursements were all linked to centralised platforms. Many citizens accepted these controls not because they were ideologically aligned, but because the alternative—being cut off from essential services—was unthinkable. Once again, exit was not prohibited; it was simply rendered terrifying.

Financial dependency is not merely technical or institutional—it is deeply emotional. It taps into core human fears: the fear of being cast out, of becoming irrelevant, of being unable to provide for oneself or one's family. These fears are primal. And systems that exploit them don't need to threaten punishment. They only need to ensure that the prospect of independence feels isolating, exhausting, and vaguely irresponsible.

This is perhaps the most insidious feature of modern dependency: it is moralised. Opting out is often portrayed not just as impractical, but as antisocial. Pay in cash, and you're an outlier. Question centralised policy, and you're a conspiracy theorist. Use privacy tools, and you're hiding something. The system does not criminalise dissent—it delegitimises it. It reframes sovereignty as selfishness, autonomy as aggression. In doing so, it recasts compliance as virtue. Fear becomes not only a functional deterrent, but a moral one.

Of course, there is a counterargument to be made: that these systems are necessary, that they provide structure and trust, and that exits *should* be difficult if they risk enabling harm. And it's true—some regulation is essential. Fraud is real. Crime exists. But when the *default assumption* is that decentralised or independent action is inherently suspicious, the system is no longer protecting citizens. It is infantilising them.

The key, then, is to distinguish between *protective interdependence* and *coercive dependency*. The former is built on transparency, consent, and recourse. The latter is built on opacity, inertia, and fear. Unfortunately, many modern financial systems are trending towards the latter—especially as digitisation and surveillance technologies converge.

Escaping this dynamic requires more than just technical solutions. It requires psychological and philosophical recalibration. Individuals must first *notice* the fear—recognise when the impulse to comply is not driven by logic, but by the dread of exclusion. Then they must examine the structures that reinforce that fear. What assumptions have been internalised? What stories are being told about what is "safe," "normal," or "mature"? Who benefits when dissent is framed as dysfunction?

From there, practical strategies become possible. Not wholesale rejection, but *deliberate disentanglement.* Building pockets of financial sovereignty: cash reserves, decentralised accounts, hard assets, skill-based barter networks. Reclaiming informational privacy. Creating community structures where legitimacy is earned through trust, not platform authorisation. These are not paranoid acts. They are the rational behaviours of people who refuse to be governed by fear alone.

In the end, the goal is not to destroy systems, but to detoxify them. To build alternatives where choice is real, and where the cost of exit is not your sense of safety, belonging, or identity. That requires courage, clarity, and above all—*consciousness.* Because the great risk of fear-based dependency is not just that we will become captives. It is that we will forget we were ever free to leave.

Chapter 2
The Psychology of Seizure

To grasp the true vulnerability of modern wealth, one must look beyond legal frameworks, institutional scaffolding, and the technological circuitry that keeps it all humming. These are the visible layers—the parts we can point to, quantify, and perhaps even trust. But the more potent forces lie buried, tucked beneath portfolios and pension plans, in places not easily charted. At the root of most financial behaviour is not a calculation, but a belief. A belief that continuity will hold, that protection will be honoured, and that—despite mounting fragility—the system will remain intact, at least in our corner of it.

This chapter concerns itself not with the architecture you can see, but with the one you carry inside: the psychological wiring that shapes our trust in financial systems. It's about how fear, denial, and the residue of personal history often override logic, even in the most educated and materially secure among us. People don't lean on institutions because they've thoroughly vetted their robustness—they do so because doubt is emotionally expensive. We tell ourselves we're being pragmatic, but underneath it all is a quieter, more primal need: the longing to feel safe.

The chain reaction that leads to loss or confiscation rarely begins with a dramatic event. It starts earlier—in quieter times, through the choices we normalise. Where we park our cash. The savings defaults we don't question. The retirement vehicles we opt into by default. These aren't idle moves. They're acts of faith. Implicitly, we enter into a bargain: you—government, employer, fund manager—look after this for me, and I won't probe too deeply.

And yet, in modern finance, safety isn't a given. It's a performance. Marketed with polished brochures, wrapped in reassuring language, and validated by historical inertia. People who'd never take a new drug without reading the fine print routinely entrust their life's savings to mechanisms they don't begin to understand. When these systems stutter—or fail outright—the damage isn't merely numeric.

It strikes at identity, at worldview. The internal monologue pivots quickly from "This is impossible" to "How did I not see it coming?"

Consider the mythology of institutional insurance. Many depositors—especially in the West—sleep easy under the impression that their funds are "insured." The word itself evokes actuarial rigour, probabilistic discipline, and moral assurance. But dig deeper. In the United States, the FDIC promises to cover accounts up to $250,000. Fair enough. But the reserves backing that guarantee, relative to total deposits, are razor-thin. In a real systemic event, repayment would hinge less on financial solvency and more on political will. Elsewhere, guarantees are even more tenuous. Yet the belief persists.

It's not just the result of clever branding or government spin. It's rooted in something older and more human: the way our minds process risk. The brain, evolutionarily speaking, isn't well equipped to deal with low-probability, high-impact threats. It seeks familiar patterns, leans toward comfort, and often projects onto institutions the traits of trusted parental figures—stability, protection, foresight. That trust isn't earned so much as assigned. Banks, state schemes, even central banks—these aren't merely economic actors. They become psychological placeholders, offering us permission to stop worrying.

This emotional outsourcing shows up most sharply in the shadows of wealth trauma. Here, personal history—especially early-life exposure to financial chaos—exerts its quiet but lasting influence. The adult whose family once lost everything to a failed investment or currency devaluation may now hoard cash obsessively or cling to government schemes with near-religious faith. These aren't strategic decisions. They're protective rituals. The pension, in such a framework, becomes not just a savings tool but a monument to perceived order. When such structures collapse, the wound is psychological as much as financial. It's not merely a question of losing assets; it's a rupture in one's internalised sense of security.

Behavioural economists and psychologists have long explored this terrain. Kahneman's work on anchoring and status quo bias shows how tenaciously people cling to existing structures. In finance, this shows up as inertia: a persistent unwillingness to question basic assumptions. The system worked yesterday, it'll probably work tomorrow. The pension fund will pay. The bank will be there. The state will step in. Even whispering the opposite feels subversive, bordering on madness. And so, denial becomes a kind of invisible scaffolding—one that holds everything in place, until it doesn't.

Denial is a seductive shield. It enables people to live within a system they privately distrust. They absorb the headlines—soaring debt, unstable currencies, creeping inflation—but compartmentalise them. The knowledge remains abstract, cordoned off from real decisions. It's easier that way. The discomfort of action—of rethinking, reallocating, restructuring—is greater than the discomfort of passive anxiety. And so, the habit holds.

But denial, while tolerable in calm conditions, exacts a brutal toll when crisis hits. Financial systems, when they fracture, tend to do so without warning. Liquidity vanishes. Trust evaporates. The very individuals who once scoffed at gold bugs or crypto advocates are found refreshing bank apps, standing in queues, or desperately trying to transfer funds that can no longer be moved. The sense of betrayal is twofold: one feels deceived by the institutions, but also by one's former certainties.

And then there is the social penalty for acting early. It's one thing to privately entertain doubts. It's another to act on them. To shift assets offshore. To diversify into alternative stores of value. To self-custody. These actions can feel socially subversive—paranoid, even. One risks not just criticism, but isolation. Among colleagues, friends, even family, such moves can be read as distrustful, eccentric, or unnecessarily severe. But those who wait often find that, by the time mainstream opinion catches up, their options have narrowed.

This chapter moves through that uncomfortable psychological territory. Not to dismiss the urge for safety, nor to vilify trust—but to illuminate the emotional circuitry behind financial behaviour. Much of what passes for "strategy" is, in truth, a form of trauma response. The sheen of stability often conceals structural vulnerability. And denial, though soothing in the short term, slowly dulls both insight and agency.

It also takes a closer look at the language of reassurance—those carefully constructed phrases like "too big to fail" or "state-guaranteed"—and how they operate more as pacifiers than disclosures. Media narratives, official statements, even expert commentary frequently serve to contain fear, not catalyse critical thought. This isn't always nefarious; often, it's reflexive—a shared cultural instinct to avoid panic. But at a certain point, reassurance becomes a form of negligence.

Still, this isn't a manifesto for doom. It's an invitation—to awareness, to agency, to the rebuilding of a more resilient financial posture. If fear is the substrate of the seizure mindset, then its counterforce isn't bravado. It's clarity. The quiet clarity that comes from recognising your psychological defaults and choosing not to be ruled by them.

True safety, the kind that can weather storms, isn't found in blind allegiance or inherited belief. It's constructed, patiently and with rigour—through choices that are both emotionally informed and strategically sound. Because as the financial world grows more entangled, more digitised, more abstracted from common sense, understanding the psychology beneath it all becomes not just useful, but essential.

In the end, this chapter isn't just about protecting capital. It's about reclaiming authorship—over your assets, yes, but also over the narrative you build around them. A narrative rooted not in illusion or inertia, but in conscious design.

Why We Obey Financial Tyranny

When bank accounts are frozen without trial, when savings are seized through executive decree, or when citizens are told their funds are inaccessible "for their own good," the natural question is: *why do people tolerate it?* One might assume that such blatant overreach would provoke mass resistance. Yet, historically and consistently, the opposite occurs. Individuals comply. Populations rationalise. Societies adapt. Financial repression, no matter how egregious, rarely triggers revolt. It triggers paperwork, queues, polite complaints—and, more often than not, self-blame.

This phenomenon is not rooted in cowardice or ignorance. It is the product of powerful psychological forces—cognitive biases, social incentives, and deep-seated trust fallacies—that make financial tyranny not only tolerable but, in many cases, invisible. The human mind is not designed for sustained vigilance against authority. It is optimised for survival within systems, not opposition to them. And when those systems manage our money, livelihoods, and access to essentials, the drive to obey becomes stronger than the instinct to rebel.

The first layer of this obedience lies in cognitive architecture. Human beings exhibit an array of mental shortcuts—heuristics—that prioritise immediate certainty over abstract risk. *Status quo bias*, for instance, inclines individuals to stick with existing arrangements even when better alternatives are available. Faced with the idea of moving assets, challenging authority, or embracing financial independence, the average person defers to familiarity. The discomfort of change outweighs the potential benefits, especially when the threat is future-oriented or probabilistic.

Closely related is *normalcy bias*, the tendency to believe that because something hasn't happened before (to *me*, in *my* country), it won't happen at all. This bias underpins the widespread faith in institutions that have previously functioned well—even when evidence suggests that stability is eroding. Argentinians who had already lived through multiple currency collapses were still stunned by the capital controls of 2001. Cypriots were shocked when bank deposits were expropriated to fund a bailout. Americans continue to treat FDIC limits as inviolable law, rather than politically contingent policy.

But even when people intellectually understand the risks, another force takes hold: *authority bias*. We are primed, from childhood, to defer to figures of power. In financial contexts, this deference is compounded by the complexity of modern systems. Few people fully grasp how fractional reserve banking works, or how central banks manipulate liquidity. And when complexity intersects with hierarchy, the result is a learned helplessness: *they must know what they're doing.* In moments of crisis, this translates into fatalistic compliance.

This is further reinforced by social proof. Most people do not make financial decisions in isolation—they model their behaviour on peers. If everyone continues to bank with the same institution, invest in the same pension schemes, or trust the same central authority, the individual is unlikely to defect, even when uneasy. Social consensus substitutes for due diligence. And when things go wrong, the collective nature of the damage creates a perverse form of comfort: *at least I wasn't alone.*

The obedience is also sustained through moral coding. Modern financial systems have moralised compliance. Paying taxes, reporting income, using regulated institutions—these are not just legal obligations; they are signals of civic virtue. To question these norms is to court suspicion. Those who move capital across borders, use alternative currencies, or self-custody wealth are framed not as prudent, but as evasive or antisocial. This framing is deliberate. It disincentivises autonomy by linking it to deviance.

Governments and financial institutions understand this dynamic intuitively. That is why they rarely use overt force to impose control. Instead, they construct narratives of *benevolent necessity.* When accounts are frozen, it is to "protect the financial system." When capital is restricted, it is to "prevent criminal activity." When access is limited, it is "for the common good." The language is paternalistic—soft, administrative, and strategically vague. It creates the illusion of care, even as it curtails freedom.

The psychological effect is powerful. Individuals facing asset seizure or restriction often internalise the justification. They wonder if they triggered it by accident. They assume there must be a good reason. They tell themselves it will be resolved soon. This is not naïveté—it is a defence mechanism. Accepting that the system has turned against you is existentially destabilising. It is easier to believe that the disruption is temporary, that the process is fair, or that you're at fault. The alternative—that you are financially powerless within a system you trusted—is too corrosive for the psyche to sustain without profound upheaval.

And so people obey. They file appeals, fill out forms, and wait for callbacks. They queue quietly at banks that have locked their funds. They refresh web portals that display zeros. They do not riot. They do not withdraw early. They do not prepare in advance. To prepare is to admit that the system might fail them. And most would rather risk loss than carry the psychological weight of suspicion.

There are historical precedents for this obedience, many of them chilling. During the 1933 gold confiscation in the United States, the vast majority of citizens turned in their bullion voluntarily—even though no meaningful enforcement existed for most. During Weimar Germany's hyperinflation, millions continued using Reichsmarks long after it was clear they had become worthless. In Zimbabwe's collapse, in Venezuela's controlled markets, in Lebanon's banking implosion—the pattern holds. People comply until the system breaks, and often long after.

Part of this obedience stems from the illusion of recourse. Systems create rituals of accountability—complaint channels, ombudsman offices, appeal processes—not necessarily to deliver justice, but to delay dissent. These mechanisms provide a sense of being heard, even when outcomes are predetermined. They turn outrage into administration. And by absorbing individual complaints into procedural mazes, they prevent collective mobilisation.

But perhaps the deepest reason we obey is that *financial systems mediate meaning*. They are not just mechanisms for storing or transmitting value; they are embedded in our sense of self. Your net worth, your credit score, your pension projections—these are identity markers.

To reject the system is not just to risk capital. It is to unsettle the narrative you've built around security, success, and even morality.

So what, then, is the antidote to this obedience? Not paranoia. Not reckless independence. But *lucid awareness*—an understanding that trust in financial systems should be earned, not assumed; that compliance should be strategic, not reflexive. It begins with questioning the narratives that surround safety: *Who told you your funds were insured? Under what conditions?* It continues with cultivating alternatives—structures of value, custody, and transaction that do not rely on a single point of failure. And it matures with community—shared knowledge, decentralised support networks, and cross-border coordination that make non-compliance less isolating.

To be clear, this is not a call to abandon systems, but to re-negotiate our relationship with them. *Obedience should be a choice, not a default.* When people understand the forces that shape their deference—when they see how fear, bias, and social pressure are exploited—they begin to reclaim agency. And that agency is the true antidote to financial tyranny. Not escape, but empowerment. Not suspicion for its own sake, but clarity that leads to sovereignty.

Because the real danger is not that systems fail. It's that when they do, *you realise too late that you were never allowed to leave.*

The Myth of Safety

The architecture of modern finance is not built on gold or concrete or reserves—it is built on confidence. This confidence, in turn, is often anchored to a triad of institutional promises: deposit insurance schemes like the FDIC, national pension systems, and the implicit invincibility of "too big to fail" institutions. These mechanisms are presented as safeguards—pillars of security in a complex, unpredictable financial landscape. But their true function is more psychological than structural. *They are not guarantees of protection; they are instruments of belief.* And belief, as history has shown, is not always a reliable foundation for safety.

The average citizen rarely questions these constructs. FDIC insurance, for example, is treated as a financial law of nature. In the United States, it promises to protect up to $250,000 per depositor, per bank, in the event of institutional failure. But few ask what underpins that guarantee, or whether it could be honoured in a systemic crisis. The Deposit Insurance Fund (DIF) is not a vault filled with enough capital to cover the entire banking system; it is a finite pool, backed by the government's ability to borrow or print money in extremis. In stable times, the fund's modest size is sufficient to resolve isolated failures. But in the context of widespread contagion—where multiple mid-sized or large institutions falter simultaneously—the scheme becomes a political triage tool, not a financial backstop.

Consider the 2008 financial crisis. Despite reassurances, the panic that gripped markets led to the temporary blanket guarantee of all bank deposits—not just those under the official FDIC limit. This was not a planned policy; it was an emergency improvisation designed to prevent collapse. The U.S. government acted not out of contractual obligation but political necessity. Similarly, in the United Kingdom, the collapse of Northern Rock in 2007 forced the government to guarantee retail deposits well beyond the statutory limit to prevent a full-scale bank run. These were ad hoc interventions—contingent, reactive, and precedent-setting. They revealed what few were willing to admit: that *deposit insurance is not an immutable safety net but a confidence mechanism, activated selectively and politically.*

Pension systems offer a parallel illusion. Across the developed world, national retirement schemes are built on pay-as-you-go models, where today's contributions fund today's retirees. These systems function not as true savings vehicles, but as intergenerational transfer programmes. Their solvency depends on favourable demographic trends, robust labour markets, and sustainable fiscal policies—conditions that are increasingly absent in ageing economies with declining birth rates and growing life expectancy.

Take the Social Security system in the United States. Official projections show that by the mid-2030s, the programme will be able to pay only around 75–80% of scheduled benefits unless significant reforms are made. Similar warning signs are flashing across European systems, including Germany, France, and Italy, where public pension obligations are approaching unsustainable proportions relative to GDP. In Japan, where over 28% of the population is over 65, the strain on the public pension system is acute and well-documented. Yet public discourse continues to treat these systems as sacrosanct, their promises inviolate. *The assumption is not that they are well-funded—it is that the government will "do something" when the time comes.*

That "something" typically involves a combination of benefit reductions, tax increases, inflationary adjustments, or delayed eligibility—none of which feel like safety from the perspective of the individual contributor. The silent transformation of a defined-benefit promise into a politically adjustable liability is rarely acknowledged until it's too late. Safety, in this context, becomes a moving target—redefined by actuarial necessity rather than contractual clarity.

The third pillar of perceived financial protection—the doctrine of "too big to fail"—is perhaps the most misleading. It suggests that certain institutions are so systemically important that their collapse would be prevented at any cost. This idea was embedded into the global psyche during the 2008 crisis, when banks like Citigroup and insurance giants like AIG received unprecedented government bailouts. The implicit message: as long as you're inside the biggest institutions, you're safe.

But this assumption contains a critical fallacy. "Too big to fail" is not a commitment to your deposits or investments. It is a strategy to preserve the broader system. The bailouts were structured to stabilise liquidity, shore up interbank lending, and prevent cascading failures—not to protect individuals. Shareholders were diluted. Bondholders took haircuts. Some firms, like Lehman Brothers, were allowed to collapse entirely. The line between who is rescued and who is sacrificed is not drawn by fairness or policy consistency. It is drawn by the logic of systemic containment.

Moreover, the post-2008 regulatory regime—while introducing stress tests, capital requirements, and resolution frameworks—has not eliminated the risk of failure. It has simply reshaped its appearance. The global financial system is now more concentrated, more complex, and more interconnected than before. Systemic risk has not been reduced; it has been redistributed. In many cases, it has migrated from the visible balance sheets of banks to the murkier world of shadow banking, derivatives markets, and sovereign debt.

This reality demands a reframing. Institutional promises are not guarantees; they are contingent liabilities. Their enforceability depends on legal architecture, fiscal capacity, political stability, and, above all, narrative control. As long as the public believes in their permanence, they function as intended. But when confidence wavers, the true nature of these mechanisms becomes apparent—they are backstops of last resort, not first-line defences.

Philosophically, the myth of safety serves a deeper function. It allows individuals to outsource responsibility. It permits the comforting fiction that someone else is managing risk. It embeds a psychological contract: *if I play by the rules, the system will protect me.* But this contract is not mutual. When the system fails—through inflation, seizure, or collapse—it does not offer reparations. It offers rationalisations: that the crisis was unforeseeable, that everyone suffered equally, that the real blame lies elsewhere.

The most dangerous consequence of this myth is not the financial loss itself. It is the erosion of agency. When people discover that their perceived safety was illusory, they often respond not with strategic adaptation but with fatalism. They feel duped. Betrayed. Paradoxically, this disempowerment often leads them to double down on the system that failed them, out of fear that there is nowhere else to go.

But there *are* alternatives. Sovereignty in financial life does not require rejecting all systems, but it does require recognising their limits. It requires diversifying *not just across asset classes, but across custodial models, jurisdictions, and trust assumptions.* It requires cultivating resilience—not the resilience that depends on the next government bailout, but the kind built through self-custody, mobility, and informed scepticism.

Safety is not the absence of risk. It is the presence of *preparedness.* And that preparedness begins with dismantling illusions. To believe that the FDIC, the pension board, or the central bank will save you under all conditions is not prudence—it is a learned dependency. It is a belief born of decades of relative stability, reinforced by narrative repetition, and sustained by the psychological comfort of conformity.

Yet history is replete with moments when the guarantees failed—when currencies were redenominated, when entitlements were slashed, when "safe" institutions imploded. These are not relics of some distant past. They are features of a cyclical pattern: overconfidence, crisis, recalibration. The people who thrive in these cycles are not the most compliant. They are the most clear-eyed.

This clarity does not come from cynicism. It comes from intellectual honesty. From asking uncomfortable questions. From recognising that what is marketed as safety is often just *deferred fragility*. And from understanding that real security begins the moment you stop expecting someone else to provide it.

The myth of safety persists because it is emotionally useful. But emotional utility is a poor substitute for structural integrity. As systems grow more complex, more indebted, and more centralised, the cost of that myth becomes harder to ignore. Eventually, the narrative cracks. The question is whether you will be positioned to adapt—or paralysed by your previous trust.

To live without illusions is not to live in fear. It is to make decisions with eyes open. And in the financial world, that is the closest thing to safety that exists.

Wealth Trauma and Emotional Hoarding

Money is never just money. It is memory. It is emotion. It is identity, agency, safety, and fear. For all the rational frameworks we apply to finance—portfolio theory, market logic, risk assessments—what often drives behaviour beneath the surface is something far less tidy: unprocessed emotional history. *Wealth trauma*—the psychological imprint of financial instability, loss, or betrayal—shapes how individuals save, spend, trust, and hoard. And when it goes unexamined, it distorts the ability to protect or grow wealth in a changing world.

Trauma in this context doesn't require catastrophe. It can emerge from events as dramatic as a currency collapse or as subtle as growing up in a household where money was a source of shame, volatility, or control. It can stem from childhood scarcity, bankruptcy, family disputes, or watching a parent silently surrender autonomy to a system they feared but relied upon. And because financial trauma is rarely acknowledged, let alone discussed openly, its patterns often play out invisibly—hidden beneath rational justifications and dressed up as "prudence," "discipline," or "conservatism."

This is how wealth trauma evolves into emotional hoarding. Just as someone who has experienced famine may hoard food long after hunger is a threat, individuals with financial trauma may engage in compulsive behaviours that reflect past fear more than present conditions. The behaviour might be excessive saving without purpose, an irrational reluctance to invest, or an aversion to spending even when needs are real. Others may bury wealth in complex financial structures they don't understand, not for strategy, but for emotional insulation—*if I can't see it, I can't lose it.*

Psychologists recognise these behaviours as trauma responses. They are not errors in judgment, but adaptations—strategies once necessary for survival, now maladaptive in new contexts. They serve a psychological purpose: control. When the external world feels unsafe, individuals attempt to create internal certainty. Money, in its quantifiable form, becomes the chosen mechanism. The account balance becomes a proxy for emotional security. The accumulation of assets, no matter how static or vulnerable, offers temporary relief from a deep-seated dread: *What if everything disappears again?*

Crucially, this is not limited to those with little money. Some of the wealthiest individuals are the most traumatised. Their wealth is not an expression of abundance, but a defence against loss. They are rich in numbers, but poor in peace. They mistrust advisors, over-diversify to the point of dilution, obsess over worst-case scenarios, and remain paralysed by the idea of financial movement. Their wealth is not a tool—it is a cage built from experience and reinforced by fear.

This is particularly evident in intergenerational patterns. A child raised by parents who lost everything—whether through war, political upheaval, market collapse, or personal failure—often inherits not just assets, but anxiety. The message may be explicit (*never trust the bank*, *cash is king*, *hide it from the government*) or implicit (*we don't talk about money*, *play it safe*, *you can't trust anyone with this*). These messages imprint early and take root deep. By adulthood, they manifest as risk aversion, secrecy, and over-dependence on traditional institutions—ironically, the very entities that may have failed the previous generation.

There is a second, subtler form of trauma that reinforces this: *institutional betrayal.* This occurs when individuals or families place trust in a system—government, bank, pension board—and are later harmed by that trust. Examples include hyperinflation that wipes out savings, expropriations, unjust tax burdens, or retirement funds lost to mismanagement. The result is not just financial damage, but existential confusion. *If the system lied to me, what can I rely on?* And yet, paradoxically, many victims of institutional betrayal return to the same systems. They double down on dependency—not because they trust again, but because the alternatives feel even more dangerous. *Better the devil you know.*

This trauma loop—betrayal followed by reluctant reattachment—is especially visible in post-crisis environments. After the 2008 financial meltdown, millions of savers who had lost wealth due to institutional recklessness poured their money right back into the same banks and markets. Why? Because the idea of withdrawing entirely was too destabilising. The system had failed, but it remained the only familiar map. Emotional hoarding is not just about clinging to money—it's about clinging to *predictability*, even if that predictability is dangerous.

We must also acknowledge how cultural narratives reinforce these patterns. Western societies often moralise wealth accumulation as a sign of virtue. Frugality becomes conflated with morality. Risk-taking is praised when it succeeds and condemned when it fails. These moral overlays make it difficult to interrogate financial behaviour honestly. A person who hoards cash out of fear may be praised as "disciplined." Someone who refuses to invest due to trauma may be seen as "conservative." The true driver—unresolved emotional distress—goes unnoticed.

Moreover, financial advice rarely engages with these dimensions. Most guidance assumes rational actors making calculated decisions based on risk and reward. But a traumatised mind does not process information through the same lens. It scans for threat, not opportunity. It seeks safety, not optimisation. The most elegant asset allocation model means little to someone who has never felt emotionally safe around money.

So what does healing look like? Not therapy alone—though psychological support can be essential—but conscious, structured financial re-education. It means separating fear from fact, and identifying which behaviours are protective and which are compulsive. It means reviewing not only one's portfolio, but the *stories* one tells about money: *Where did this belief come from? Whose fear am I carrying? What am I trying to control by refusing to act?*

It also requires building new systems of trust—ones that are earned, not inherited. For some, this might mean taking partial ownership of assets rather than outsourcing everything to third parties. For others, it might involve learning the mechanics of self-custody or rethinking diversification in terms of jurisdiction, not just asset class. These steps are not merely tactical—they are therapeutic. They replace paralysis with clarity.

There is also a communal dimension. Wealth trauma often thrives in isolation. Families don't talk about money. Partners avoid difficult conversations. Children inherit habits but not the history behind them. Breaking this pattern requires intergenerational dialogue. It requires creating spaces where money is not a taboo but a topic of mutual inquiry. Only then can the next generation inherit not just assets, but insight.

Finally, we must confront the deeper philosophical truth: *there is no such thing as permanent safety*. The pursuit of absolute security—through hoarding, freezing, or blind trust—is itself a symptom of trauma. Resilience, by contrast, does not come from denial or dependence. It comes from adaptability, agency, and a willingness to engage with uncertainty rather than hide from it.

Wealth, when governed by fear, becomes a liability. It traps rather than liberates. But when trauma is acknowledged, examined, and slowly unwound, wealth can begin to serve its proper function—not as a monument to past losses, but as a dynamic resource for present life and future possibility.

This chapter does not offer quick fixes. There are no formulas for emotional release or one-size-fits-all strategies. But it does offer a framework: a way of seeing financial behaviour not as error or eccentricity, but as encrypted autobiography. When we read that autobiography carefully—when we follow its logic rather than dismiss it—we begin to write a new script. One not rooted in scarcity, betrayal, or inherited fear, but in conscious stewardship. That, more than any account balance or insurance policy, is the foundation of enduring security.

The Cost of Denial

Few risks are more dangerous than the ones we refuse to see. And when it comes to personal finance, systemic fragility, and institutional trust, *denial is not merely a psychological blind spot—it is a quantifiable liability.* Across history and geography, the most devastating financial losses are not suffered by those who took risks, but by those who clung to assumptions: that banks would remain solvent, that currencies would hold value, that governments would honour obligations. These assumptions—seldom examined, rarely updated—form the bedrock of middle-class stability. And when they fail, they fail spectacularly.

Denial operates on multiple levels. It begins at the individual scale, where people continue to treat financial institutions, insurance guarantees, or pension systems as fixed realities, despite mounting evidence to the contrary. It extends to the societal level, where political narratives and media discourse collude—consciously or otherwise—to downplay structural rot. And it culminates in the institutional domain, where regulators and policymakers avoid hard decisions until the crisis is already irreversible. What unites all these levels is a shared psychological resistance to change, even when the cost of stasis is ruin.

At its core, denial is not the absence of information; it is the refusal to integrate that information into meaningful action. Many individuals *know* that fiat currencies inflate, that governments debase debt through monetary expansion, or that pension liabilities are outpacing contributions. Yet they continue to make plans, allocate assets, and structure their lives as if the official narratives are stable. This isn't irrational in the classic sense. It's *emotionally rational.* To truly internalise fragility would require changing behaviour, confronting discomfort, or challenging one's social and professional environment. For most people, that price feels higher than the theoretical risk of loss.

But the cost of denial accumulates silently—and it compounds. Consider the collapse of the Soviet Union in the early 1990s. For months, even as shelves emptied and hyperinflation loomed, many Soviet citizens continued to save in roubles, assuming the state would step in to stabilise purchasing power. When the government failed to deliver, life savings evaporated almost overnight. In Venezuela, similar patterns emerged. Despite years of currency devaluation, many professionals held on to bolívar-denominated assets until they became virtually worthless, because shifting to dollars was illegal, logistically complex, or socially stigmatised. The choice not to act was not rooted in ignorance—it was rooted in the *emotional gravity of denial.*

Even in advanced economies, the pattern persists. During the Cypriot banking crisis in 2013, depositors who ignored early signs of trouble—media leaks, political denials, unusual withdrawal patterns—found their accounts subject to an overnight bail-in. The confiscation was legalised after the fact. Meanwhile, those who moved early, accepting the social awkwardness and logistical burden of transferring funds abroad, were often criticised as alarmists—until they were proven prudent. *The difference between foresight and regret was measured not in knowledge, but in willingness to act.*

This unwillingness to act is frequently framed as optimism, prudence, or social trust. But more often, it reflects cognitive distortions. *Optimism bias* leads individuals to believe that negative outcomes are less likely to happen to them personally, even if they are happening to others. *Normalcy bias* convinces people that because something has not happened before—at least in living memory—it cannot happen now. *Present bias* favours immediate convenience over long-term resilience. All three converge in financial behaviour, blinding individuals to fragile structures hiding in plain sight.

This blindness is rarely challenged by institutional signals. Governments and financial institutions are structurally incentivised to preserve confidence—often at the expense of transparency. Officials downplay banking instability to avoid panic. Central banks use technocratic language to obscure monetary deterioration. Pension boards project optimistic returns to preserve the illusion of solvency. None of this is necessarily malicious. In most cases, these actors genuinely believe they are buying time for a soft landing. But from the perspective of the individual saver or investor, the result is clear: *by the time the public warning arrives, the private damage is already done.*

There is a long tradition of this delay. In 2007, Ben Bernanke famously remarked that the subprime mortgage crisis was "contained." A year later, Lehman Brothers collapsed, and the global financial system was brought to the brink. In 2023, Credit Suisse executives were still assuring investors of their capital strength days before a forced merger wiped out shareholder equity. Reassurance is the default public posture of every collapsing institution—until collapse is undeniable.

This dynamic places individuals in a difficult position. To accept fragility requires not only a reassessment of risk, but also a confrontation with social and psychological discomfort. Taking proactive steps—moving assets offshore, diversifying into hard or decentralised assets, restructuring dependency on state pensions—can feel paranoid, disloyal, or selfish. It may involve explaining difficult choices to family, risking friction with peers, or incurring short-term costs for long-term preservation. Denial, by contrast, offers ease. Until it doesn't.

The financial cost of denial is not merely a one-time loss; it often leads to *irrecoverable diminishment.* Savings evaporated by inflation cannot be replenished with modest returns. Time lost to institutional dysfunction—locked funds, delayed payments, restructured benefits—cannot be reclaimed. The psychological shock of sudden reversal often paralyses individuals, delaying their response and compounding the damage. Worse, many respond by doubling down on the system that failed them, hoping that the next cycle will restore what was lost.

Contrast this with the approach taken by those who cultivate *financial awareness* over blind confidence. These individuals do not necessarily reject the system—they use it selectively, while insulating themselves from its points of failure. They acknowledge that no institution, however venerable, is immune to erosion. They build redundancy: alternative jurisdictions, portable income, diversified custody. They are willing to ask the uncomfortable question: *what if this fails?* Not as paranoia, but as preparation.

This preparation is not simply technical; it is psychological. It involves training oneself to see fragility where others see stability, to act without consensus, and to tolerate the discomfort of being early. It means recognising that the safety of the crowd is often an illusion, and that the price of acting alone is lower than the price of reacting too late. It also means reframing prudence: *not as trust in institutions, but as clarity about their limits.*

There are, of course, trade-offs. Proactive adaptation requires effort, education, and emotional maturity. It may involve sacrifices—tax complexity, frictional costs, temporary isolation. But these are investments, not losses. They are the price of independence in a system where denial is rewarded in the short term and punished in the long term.

Ultimately, the cost of denial is not only personal. It is civilisational. When too many individuals outsource responsibility to systems they don't understand, the system itself becomes more brittle. Fragility spreads from households to institutions to governments. And when the reckoning comes, it is not the elites or the policymakers who suffer first—it is the ordinary savers, retirees, and wage earners who believed, until the last moment, that someone else was watching the risks.

This chapter is not a call to pessimism. It is a call to *conscious realism.* To reject denial is not to expect collapse—it is to prepare for volatility. It is to reclaim authorship over one's financial life, in a world where narratives are curated and warnings come too late. Denial is comfortable, until it becomes catastrophic. Awareness is difficult, until it becomes liberating.

The cost of denial is not just measured in lost money—it is measured in lost time, lost options, and lost sovereignty. The question is not whether fragility exists. It is whether you choose to see it—and act—before the system decides for you.

Chapter 3
A History of Hidden Wealth

Wealth has rarely resided where we were told to look. Nor has it ever been as secure, transparent, or equitably distributed as the mythos of modern finance insists. Across centuries, those who preserved their fortunes through currency collapses, autocratic turns, and institutional betrayals rarely did so by leaning on the rules—they did so by quietly stepping outside them. In nearly every instance where a society slid from abundance to asset seizure—through nationalisation, capital flight restrictions, runaway inflation, or official theft—there has been a quieter story beneath the headlines. A story not of alarmism, but of foresight. Of individuals who, sensing the early tremors, ignored the comforts of reassurance and moved their assets beyond the reach of the machinery that would later consume them. This chapter concerns them—and the covert architectures they built.

To study hidden wealth is not to celebrate secrecy, nor to romanticise evasion. It is, rather, to observe recurring behaviour. When a government begins to fray—when tax revenue dries up, debt becomes unserviceable, or the national currency wobbles—the pattern that emerges is almost inevitable. States do not fold neatly inward; they cannibalise. They do not relinquish power—they rewrite laws. They dip into pensions, quietly inflate away obligations, restrict capital flows, and define new thresholds of "excess" to justify appropriation. And yet, alongside this predictable pattern, another unfolds: a small subset of individuals who don't wait to be devoured. They observe. They move. They endure.

No conspiracies need to be invoked. The evidence is in the historical record—open-source, widely covered at the time, and later softened by the haze of forgetfulness. In Argentina, 2001, the government froze every bank account in the country. Withdrawal limits were set at 250 pesos a week—regardless of the balance. The rationale? To stem capital flight and protect the banking sector. The result? A wholesale seizure of public savings. Middle-class Argentinians—diligent, tax-compliant, trusting—lost access to their life's work.

Those who had quietly shifted their wealth into foreign currencies or foreign accounts were accused of disloyalty. Yet they were the ones left standing when the music stopped.

Or look to India, 2016. A late-evening broadcast from Prime Minister Modi declared 86% of the nation's currency instantly void. The declared aim: eliminating counterfeit notes and black money. But for millions—especially the poor and informal sector workers—the consequence was a sudden financial paralysis. Queues stretched for days. Cash-dependent enterprises collapsed. It wasn't the corrupt who bore the brunt, but ordinary citizens who'd trusted the permanence of their rupee holdings. Meanwhile, those who had hedged early—into gold, land, or hard assets abroad—escaped the worst of it.

Such examples abound: Weimar Germany, 1923—where banknotes piled higher than firewood; Cyprus, 2013—where uninsured deposits vanished overnight; Zimbabwe—where a fresh currency name arrived every year, alongside its inevitable obsolescence. The policies change, but the plot is painfully consistent: when a state teeters on the brink, private capital becomes its emergency ration.

What's more curious is how few people act before the breach. Not because they're uninformed—often, the warning signs accumulate in plain view—but because of a stubborn psychological bias: the refusal to believe one's government might turn predatory. Comforted by a lifetime of bureaucratic stability, citizens rationalise the tremors. They assume recovery, believe statements, and defer to authority. Meanwhile, another economy quietly emerges beneath their feet.

Indeed, the story of concealed wealth is, in effect, the story of shadow economies—parallel systems of value and trade that spring up when official ones begin to fracture. During the Soviet bloc's final years, hard Western currencies—Deutschmarks, dollars—became the real coin of survival, traded behind the curtain of the rouble. In contemporary Venezuela, U.S. dollars circulate alongside bolívars rendered useless by hyperinflation. In Lebanon, where the national currency collapsed into absurdity, families turned to gold, stablecoins, and dollar-backed real estate deals paid in envelopes of cash. These systems are not aberrations; they are the natural, perhaps inevitable, consequence of monetary systems that betray their citizens.

Crucially, these informal economies aren't always criminal. In many cases, they function with more integrity than the state-sanctioned ones—free of manipulated statistics or coercive compliance. Their legitimacy is derived from necessity, not ideology. And while many only turn to these alternatives after crisis hits, a few do so pre-emptively. They understand something essential: the first real act of financial freedom is the ability to exit.

That lesson has perhaps never been more urgent. In past decades, economic repression was visible: queues at banks, hyperinflationary price tags, or midnight decrees. But today's control mechanisms are slicker, embedded in algorithms and platforms rather than overt policy. What happens when confiscation becomes a function of code? When payment networks can be silently throttled, or accounts frozen not by courts, but by terms and conditions? When inflation is masked behind metrics, and negative real interest rates eat savings invisibly? This is the new frontier. The motifs are familiar—but the machinery has evolved.

Consider central bank digital currencies (CBDCs). On paper, they offer modernisation, inclusion, convenience. But they also introduce programmable money—trackable, censorable, and fully within institutional reach. A transaction could be denied not because it's illegal, but because it breaches a future policy. Access to funds might hinge on behaviour, geography, even social scoring. And once such a system becomes the default, opting out becomes near-impossible. Participation will not be requested—it will be assumed.

All of which renders the study of hidden wealth not a nostalgic indulgence, but a contemporary imperative. No, the answer is not buried coins or offshore secrecy. It's strategic clarity. It's understanding whether your wealth is portable, whether it can survive surveillance, and whether your financial existence is wholly dependent on the goodwill of systems that may one day fail you.

This chapter aims to cultivate that awareness—not with panic, but with precision. It seeks to map the contours of economic fragility in the digital age. To show how parallel systems evolve under stress, and why historical collapse now wears new clothes—user-friendly, cloud-based, and fully automated. We'll revisit case studies not as tales of woe, but as maps of anticipation. We'll probe the emotional mechanisms—trust, inertia, conformity—that keep people compliant even when signs are blaring. And we'll explore what it means to design a financial life with optionality baked in.

Because every crisis has two timelines. The one we read about after the fact—neatly summarised in post-mortems—and the one that lives in whispers, quiet transfers, early withdrawals. It is on that latter timeline that sovereignty is reclaimed. Not in the spirit of rebellion, but in the quiet discipline of foresight. Because once the state positions itself as your custodian, hidden wealth ceases to be subversive. It becomes your anchor of autonomy.

Gold in the Walls: Ancient Evasions

The assumption that wealth equals possession—and possession equals control—is a modern illusion. Across centuries and civilisations, ownership has always been contested, conditional, and political. When those in power decided that certain groups were enemies of the state, heretics, or merely too rich to be left alone, wealth quickly became a liability. And yet, again and again, individuals and families found ways to protect what was theirs—not by trusting laws or appealing to institutions, but by removing their wealth from visibility altogether. What today we might call asset protection, they understood intuitively: *to keep it, you must first make it unseizable.*

Throughout history, wealth has not only been stolen in wars or plundered in conquest—it has been appropriated by domestic decree. States, rulers, and revolutions have all found rationales to seize private holdings: for "the public good," for "national security," or to enforce ideological conformity. Whether under fascist, communist, colonial, or even democratic regimes, the confiscation of property has often begun not with violence, but with paperwork. First a registry, then a tax, then a seizure. Those who survived these cycles of appropriation did not simply hide—they adapted. They buried gold, repurposed heirlooms, converted liquid into labour, or transformed visible assets into trustless stores of value. And in doing so, they embedded a kind of encoded wisdom into family lineages: that the true vault is not always the bank or the law, but the imagination of those willing to think beyond them.

One of the most studied yet under-appreciated historical examples comes from Europe during the rise of Nazism. As Jewish families in Germany and Austria faced asset freezes, professional exclusion, and eventual deportation, many realised too late that their wealth was already within reach of the regime. Those who anticipated the threat—often based on instinct more than evidence—moved assets abroad, converted currency into jewels or gold, or embedded value into portable items: art, heirlooms, even household items with concealed compartments. In some cases, families literally *hid gold in the walls*—a phrase that would become tragically literal in the decades to follow, as properties were confiscated and wealth rendered unrecoverable. Post-war excavations in Berlin and Vienna continue to uncover caches—forgotten by time, lost by lineage, or never retrieved by their rightful owners.

But such evasions were not exclusive to twentieth-century Europe. Go back further, and the same patterns recur. During the French Revolution, as the Jacobins escalated property seizures against the aristocracy and church, many nobles smuggled their wealth out through coded letters, false accounts, or sympathetic foreign banks. Others embedded value into artworks or commissioned sculptures with hollow bases to hide coinage. The collapse of ancien régime France created a vacuum in which legal property became political property overnight. In that moment, those who had converted visible assets into obscured, mobile, or deniable forms of value were not merely richer—they were *safer*.

Similar instincts guided Buddhist monks and landowning families in feudal Japan during the Meiji Restoration. As centuries-old domains were restructured under imperial consolidation, hereditary rights and estate holdings evaporated. Religious institutions, once protected, found themselves disbanded or repurposed. In anticipation, several temples transformed their material wealth—statues, bells, and ceremonial vessels—into conduits for storage. Bronze Buddhas concealed coinage. Wall murals hid parchments that documented hidden land titles. Aware that government reform was often a euphemism for confiscation, these communities preserved value through cultural camouflage. In many cases, those items were never recovered—not because they were lost, but because they remained where they were never suspected.

The Roman Empire offers yet another lens. In times of political instability or external invasion, Roman elites would bury hoards of gold, silver, and currency in amphorae, jars, or underground cellars. Not out of superstition, but out of strategic prudence. These hoards were not mere savings—they were contingency reserves. Archaeological records across Britain, Gaul, and Eastern Europe have uncovered thousands of such caches, often interred around the third and fourth centuries CE, when the empire was beset by inflation, tax increases, and raids. What's instructive is not just the existence of these hidden stashes, but their volume. The sheer quantity of buried currency suggests that entire classes of citizens understood the limits of state reliability—and acted accordingly.

The impulse to protect wealth from seizures is not necessarily about greed or defiance. More often, it is about *continuity*. When regimes change, currencies collapse, or rulers turn on their own people, the ability to retain value becomes existential. It determines whether a family can flee or remain, whether generations continue in dignity or fall into destitution. Hidden wealth has financed escapes, preserved education, rebuilt businesses, and reconstituted communities. Its purpose is not just protection—it is regeneration.

And yet, not every evasion strategy succeeded. There are lessons in failure, too. Some attempts to hide assets became too elaborate, rendering wealth inaccessible even to its owners. Others failed due to overconfidence in intermediaries—trusting that a neighbour, official, or banker would protect hidden goods. Many were betrayed. Still others were caught by changes in the law itself: retroactive taxes, criminalisation of offshore accounts, or declarations of "excess wealth." These failures reveal an important truth: *secrecy is not strategy*. It is only effective when paired with foresight, redundancy, and psychological clarity.

Today, the tools are different, but the logic remains. Modern equivalents of "gold in the walls" include multisignature wallets, decentralised identity layers, and encrypted seed phrases. A hard drive buried in an orchard may now hold more wealth than a warehouse full of bullion. Yet the underlying principle—of removing assets from institutions that may turn hostile—has not changed. Nor has the psychological burden. Just as in the past, those who protect their assets today must resist the inertia of public opinion, the social pressure of conformity, and the comfort of official reassurance.

It's worth reflecting on what these ancient evasions teach us about trust. Not trust in people, but trust in systems. Across all eras, the tipping point comes not when governments lose competence, but when they lose credibility. The moment wealth becomes visible to a desperate regime is the moment it becomes vulnerable. And at that threshold, legality is irrelevant. What matters is custody—and control.

This subchapter doesn't romanticise secrecy. It clarifies its strategic role in conditions of systemic volatility. It invites readers to study ancient tactics not for imitation, but for insight. What made them work? Why did some succeed and others fail? What were the trade-offs, and how were they justified? Above all, it asks a modern reader to do what past survivors did instinctively: *see the possibility of confiscation not as paranoia, but as a structural risk*. The historical record does not suggest that wealth is protected by law. It suggests that wealth is protected by prudence, foresight, and deliberate invisibility.

Gold in the walls was never just about gold. It was about foresight in the face of fragility. And in a world increasingly digitised, surveilled, and centralised, it might be worth remembering that old techniques—though crude by today's standards—were often more secure than the systems we now call advanced.

When Nations Eat Their Own

When a government runs out of money, it rarely runs out of reach. The state, faced with a collapsing tax base, unsustainable debt, or political disintegration, does not quietly expire. It consumes. It turns inward. And when it does, it does not raid foreign treasuries or launch new industrial revolutions—it preys on its own citizens. History has shown, repeatedly and with astonishing consistency, that states in distress will default not just on bonds, but on promises, pensions, currencies, and property rights. The polite term is "crisis management." The more accurate description is *state expropriation under legal cover*. This subchapter examines how that process unfolds—not as isolated incidents, but as a structural pattern that recurs across geography, ideology, and regime type.

Consider Zimbabwe, a textbook case for students of hyperinflation. In the early 2000s, Robert Mugabe's government began an aggressive programme of land redistribution, seizing commercial farms without compensation and triggering the collapse of agricultural output. With tax revenues falling and foreign aid withdrawn, the Reserve Bank began printing money to cover deficits. By 2008, annual inflation had reached 89.7 sextillion percent. Savings were obliterated. Salaries had to be renegotiated daily. Citizens who had trusted in their currency—the Zimbabwean dollar—saw their entire net worth vanish not through theft in the traditional sense, but through a *state-sanctioned dilution of value*. To survive, people turned to barter, gold, and U.S. dollars smuggled in through informal networks. Those who had anticipated the collapse and stored value outside the currency system managed to preserve something. The rest became collateral damage in their own country's monetary failure.

But Zimbabwe is not unique. Argentina, one of the wealthiest nations per capita in the early twentieth century, has gone through *nine sovereign defaults* in its modern history. In 2001, amid a severe economic downturn, the government imposed the "corralito"—a freeze on all bank withdrawals above a minimal threshold. Overnight, millions were locked out of their own accounts. Deposits denominated in U.S. dollars were forcibly converted into devalued pesos at an unfavourable exchange rate. The legal justification was emergency stabilisation; the economic reality was mass confiscation through financial repression. The result: shattered trust, social unrest, and a multi-generational lesson in why keeping wealth inside a fragile system is not security—it's exposure.

Russia offers another striking example. After the fall of the Soviet Union, citizens were encouraged to trust the new rouble and invest in domestic bonds. In 1998, the Russian government defaulted on its debt, devalued the rouble, and froze foreign exchange markets. Bank accounts denominated in dollars were forcibly converted. Inflation surged. Trust in financial institutions evaporated overnight. And yet again, those who had diversified into hard assets—especially dollars, gold, and real estate—found themselves relatively shielded. The mechanism was different from Zimbabwe, but the effect was identical: *the state rewrote the rules of value to its own advantage, and citizens bore the loss.*

One might assume these examples are confined to unstable or authoritarian regimes. But that would be both naïve and ahistorical. The United States, often held as a model of financial maturity, offers its own precedent. In 1933, amid the Great Depression, President Franklin D. Roosevelt signed Executive Order 6102, making it illegal for American citizens to own more than a token amount of gold. All gold coinage and bullion were to be turned over to the Federal Reserve in exchange for paper dollars—at a fixed rate. A year later, the government revalued gold from $20.67 to $35 per ounce, effectively reducing the purchasing power of those dollars by 40%. This was not a marginal policy—it was the largest peacetime confiscation of private wealth in American history, executed not with force, but with signatures and stamps. Those who had stored their savings in gold, trusting it to protect them from inflation, were retroactively criminalised.

The logic behind these moves is always the same: *extraordinary times require extraordinary measures*. And the justifications are dressed in patriotic, moral, or technocratic language: "to preserve economic stability," "to prevent a run on the banks," "to ensure fairness in distribution." But beneath the rhetoric lies a recurring truth—when a nation is financially cornered, it no longer distinguishes between protection and predation. Wealth becomes a resource to be tapped, not respected. The state becomes a competitor, not a guarantor.

Nor are such tactics purely historical. In 2013, Cyprus became the first eurozone country to impose a "bail-in" as part of its bank rescue plan. Rather than bailing out banks with taxpayer money, the government decided that *depositors themselves*—those with more than €100,000 in Cypriot bank accounts—would take the hit. Up to 60% of deposits were seized in exchange for shares in the failing banks. It was a stunning precedent: insured deposits were safe; uninsured deposits were retroactively reclassified as *risk-bearing capital.* This was no banana republic—it was a member of the European Union. And it marked a shift in global financial norms: the idea that your bank account might be treated as a funding source in systemic distress was no longer theoretical. It had become policy.

What makes these events so insidious is their *predictable denial.* Before every crisis, officials assert that the fundamentals are strong, the institutions sound, the safety nets adequate. Warnings are dismissed as alarmist, or worse, unpatriotic. The public, primed by decades of system trust and short financial memory, continues to store wealth in local banks, in local currency, on the assumption that *if something were truly wrong, someone would have told them*. And by the time reality breaks through, the doors are already locked—often literally.

It is worth noting that these crises don't always announce themselves with chaos. Sometimes the theft is slow, cumulative, and hidden in the numbers. Consider negative real interest rates—where inflation quietly outpaces returns on savings. In effect, the state funds itself by eroding the value of citizen deposits. It's a form of financial repression: no outright seizure, no capital controls, but a steady confiscation through manipulated incentives. Over time, the effect is the same as a more dramatic confiscation—it just feels less scandalous.

There is a philosophical point buried in all this: *legality is not the same as legitimacy*. Many of the most impactful acts of wealth confiscation have been perfectly legal—passed by parliaments, signed by presidents, rubber-stamped by courts. The fact that an act is legal does not mean it is just, and certainly not that it is safe to ignore. This distinction is essential for modern asset protection. It requires a mindset shift: away from *trust in systems* toward *trust in structure*. Not where the wealth is, but *how it is held*. Not whether the laws are clear, but whether the custodians have the incentive and the capacity to honour them in crisis.

To understand how nations eat their own is to recognise a structural truth about wealth and power: *when the latter is threatened, the former is expendable*. There is no such thing as a permanent rule of law under fiscal duress. There are only temporary agreements between the powerful and the governed—agreements which can be revised without notice, justified after the fact, and reversed at will. Anyone seeking financial sovereignty must not only understand this history but internalise its implications.

This subchapter is not about fear—it is about foresight. It presents hard evidence that the line between order and confiscation is thinner than most realise, and that the best defence is not outrage after the fact, but proactive insulation before the crisis. The strategy is not to escape systems entirely, but to ensure that your exposure to them is always discretionary. Because the question is not *whether* a modern nation will once again eat its own—it is *who will be on the menu when it does.*

The Rise of the Parallel Economy

When formal economies collapse, informal ones awaken—not as acts of rebellion, but as acts of survival. The parallel economy is not a symptom of lawlessness; it is a response to law failing to deliver on its promises. When a government can no longer provide stable currency, functional markets, or credible institutions, the citizenry does not wait for reform—it reconfigures trust. New systems of exchange emerge, often rooted in relationships rather than regulation, in goods rather than fiat, and in necessity rather than legality. These underground economies are not fringe phenomena. They become the *core architecture* of economic life when the official system is hollowed out. Understanding them is not a matter of exotic curiosity—it is essential preparation for anyone who hopes to safeguard value in an unstable world.

One of the clearest contemporary illustrations is Venezuela. Over the past two decades, the country has moved from a relatively prosperous petrostate to a failed monetary experiment. As inflation soared into the millions of percent and the bolívar became practically worthless, conventional banking, commerce, and employment structures collapsed. Yet Venezuelans continued to eat, trade, and communicate. How? The black market became the default market. U.S. dollars, once restricted by law, became the de facto currency in cities. Barter systems emerged in rural areas, where food, fuel, and medicine became currency. Peer-to-peer messaging apps like WhatsApp served as platforms for informal contracting. Children sold foreign gum for tips in hard currency. Families wired remittances in bitcoin or USDT (a dollar-pegged stablecoin), then used local brokers to convert them discreetly. The state lost control over monetary policy, but society did not disintegrate. It *reorganised.*

Zimbabwe offers another telling case. During its most extreme inflationary spiral in the 2000s, people quickly lost faith in the formal economy. Supermarkets had empty shelves, while roadside vendors had fresh produce. Fuel stations operated only for those with access to foreign currency or connections. The official banking sector became unusable, not just because of capital controls and liquidity issues, but because its entire value proposition—safe storage, legal recourse, currency stability—had collapsed. What took its place were *trust networks*: family-to-family exchanges, diaspora-backed micro-economies, and barter-based marketplaces. Eggs could buy bread; phone credit could buy cooking oil. The rule was simple: if it worked, it spread—regardless of whether it was legal or taxed.

The lesson here is not that state institutions are irrelevant, but that they are *replaceable* when they cease to function. Economists often frame informal economies as inefficient or criminal. But in times of systemic failure, they are often more accurate indicators of actual economic health than official metrics. Consider Greece during its 2010–2015 debt crisis. As austerity measures crippled spending and tax collection efforts intensified, the informal economy surged—estimated at over 25% of GDP. Islanders in Ikaria reportedly returned to barter for basic services. In Athens, families began offering medical care in exchange for repairs, or renting flats in bitcoin to bypass capital controls. It wasn't criminality—it was *parallel adaptation.* The legal system had failed to meet basic needs; parallel systems emerged that could.

These examples underscore a deeper point: *currency is not money, and regulation is not trust.* People do not stop transacting when their banking app stops working. They simply reroute the trust channel. In Argentina, where inflation and currency crises are routine, citizens have developed a sophisticated instinct for financial survival. Many keep their savings in U.S. dollars—physically stored or digitally held via stablecoins. Real estate transactions are frequently done in cash, with contracts often honoured more through social enforcement than state backing. The peso may be the official unit, but the economy speaks in dollars, gold, or favours. The parallel economy is not fringe—it is embedded in the culture, a reflex developed through repeated betrayal.

One of the most significant developments in recent years is the digitisation of the parallel economy. Historically, underground markets were constrained by geography and trust limitations. But technology has changed that calculus. In Nigeria, for instance, when the government banned the use of crypto for financial institutions, peer-to-peer platforms exploded. People bypassed the formal financial rails entirely. They used Telegram groups and WhatsApp chains to trade USDT for naira, coordinate remittance flows, and even negotiate contract labour across borders. The government's ban, far from crushing the market, simply pushed it into a more decentralised, less visible form. The grid lost legitimacy; the street gained encryption.

This is not limited to developing countries. In Canada, during the 2022 trucker protests, the federal government invoked emergency powers to freeze bank accounts of protest organisers and donors. Regardless of one's political stance, the precedent was clear: *compliance with government objectives became a condition for financial access*. In response, bitcoin wallets—especially those held via privacy-preserving tools like CoinJoin or multisig—became central to sustaining donations. The infrastructure of the parallel economy was deployed not in a failed state, but in a G7 nation. The lesson: when trust in institutions breaks, alternatives don't have to be invented from scratch—they already exist.

What, then, defines a parallel economy? It is not merely "illegal activity." Rather, it is any system of value exchange that operates *outside the exclusive control of the state.* This includes grey markets, barter systems, community currencies, crypto networks, and unregistered service exchanges. These systems thrive on *resilience, adaptability, and decentralised trust.* They are harder to tax, harder to surveil, and—most importantly—harder to shut down. They often emerge spontaneously, but they endure because they solve real problems in environments where the state has failed to do so.

Yet there are risks. Parallel economies lack consumer protections, standardised enforcement, and clear dispute resolution. They often rely on interpersonal trust, which can be abused. The absence of regulation means the presence of opportunists. But these are not arguments against parallel economies—they are *realities to be navigated within them.* Just as one would not walk into a volatile stock market blindfolded, one should not romanticise underground economies. But one should also not ignore them. They are a survival mechanism with a long historical pedigree, not a new-age experiment.

From medieval trade guilds that issued their own tokens, to black markets in Soviet Russia where American jeans were currency, to decentralised autonomous organisations (DAOs) funding projects via crypto today—*humans have always created economic order outside formal structures when those structures became untrustworthy.* The terminology may change; the underlying psychology does not.

For those thinking about asset protection, sovereignty, and financial resilience, the rise of the parallel economy is not a marginal concern. It is a crucial model. It shows that *value can move, grow, and be preserved without institutional approval.* That is not a revolutionary idea—it is a defensive one. When systems become extractive, fragile, or adversarial, adaptation is not disobedience. It is prudence.

The parallel economy is not an alternative to the future. It *is* the future for those who understand that financial sovereignty begins where institutional trust ends. In a world where digitisation makes freezing easier than fleeing, and where compliance is increasingly baked into financial architecture, the capacity to *exit*—quietly, flexibly, and without triggering alarms—becomes a core competency. The underground, once stigmatised, is now a laboratory. Those who study it today will not just survive tomorrow. They will *shape* what replaces the formal economy when it falters.

History Doesn't Repeat, It Upgrades

The mechanisms by which wealth is seized, tracked, or denied access have never been static. They have always evolved in lockstep with the dominant technologies of the age. From Roman tax records chiselled into marble to Cold War-era bank freezes, state power has long adapted itself to the infrastructure available. But today, something profoundly different is happening: *the tools of financial repression are no longer merely bureaucratic—they are algorithmic.* The systems once used to safeguard commerce have become the very architecture through which control is enforced. And unlike the blunt instruments of the past—such as physical raids or currency confiscation—modern systems operate invisibly, silently, and at scale. Control has gone digital, and with that shift, the nature of the threat has transformed.

To understand this evolution, it's useful to start with the analogue forms of financial coercion. In 1933, during the depths of the Great Depression, the United States government issued Executive Order 6102, criminalising the private ownership of gold. Citizens were compelled to turn over their bullion to the Federal Reserve in exchange for paper dollars, under threat of imprisonment and hefty fines. This was a direct, overt act of wealth seizure justified under the guise of economic stabilisation. It required physical enforcement: vaults opened, homes searched, assets physically transported. It was dramatic, visible, and limited in reach.

Fast forward to the 21st century, and we see a parallel development—but vastly more efficient. In 2022, when Russia invaded Ukraine, Western nations responded with sweeping financial sanctions. Russian state assets held in European and U.S.

banks were frozen overnight. Oligarchs' yachts were impounded, corporate accounts locked, and transactions in major currencies halted. These actions did not require raids, armies, or even new legislation. They required *back-end administrative access*—the digital keys to the global banking system. Wealth vanished from utility not because it was stolen, but because it was rendered inert. *The asset didn't need to be moved; it only needed to be permissioned.*

This distinction matters. In the modern context, ownership is less about possession and more about *access*. If you cannot move your money, spend it, or transmit it—regardless of whether it has your name on it—it is, functionally, no longer yours. And access today is largely mediated by software. Your banking app is not merely a window into your finances—it is a gatekeeper. If an algorithm flags your transaction as suspicious, a freeze can be automatic. If a regulation changes overnight, your funds can be reclassified. When systems are coded for control, the difference between asset protection and asset prison becomes a matter of software architecture.

Consider the rise of "debanking." In recent years, individuals and organisations—often without criminal charges—have found their accounts closed without explanation. In the UK, several high-profile figures discovered that their accounts were being terminated due to reputational or political concerns. One such case involved Nigel Farage, whose personal and business accounts with Coutts Bank were shut down. While the bank initially cited commercial grounds, internal documents later revealed concerns about Farage's political views and "alignment with corporate values." This is a textbook example of financial infrastructure being weaponised not through due process, but through *risk modelling and internal optics*. The digital rails of the economy are no longer neutral; they are curators.

Historically, power was centralised through physical monopolies: control of minting, taxation, or military force. But today, financial centralisation is algorithmic. The central bank digital currency

(CBDC) is the clearest modern manifestation of this trend. Advocates argue that CBDCs will offer efficiency, transparency, and inclusion. But critics—and anyone with a sense of historical pattern recognition—see the darker possibility: programmable money. A CBDC can, by design, be limited in scope, time, or geography. It can be coded to prevent purchase of certain items, expire after a set period, or be geofenced to disallow cross-border usage. This is not a hypothetical; China's digital yuan already contains elements of such programmability. What gold seizures achieved with physical force in 1933, programmable money can now achieve through a line of code.

Importantly, this is not to imply a vast conspiracy or inevitable dystopia. It is to recognise that the *design of financial systems reflects the incentives of those who build and operate them.* In an era of data-driven governance, "compliance" becomes less about adhering to law and more about conforming to constantly evolving behavioural norms. If your spending patterns deviate from expected norms, you may be flagged. If your political donations fall outside the consensus, you may be restricted. The system doesn't need to understand your intentions. It only needs to identify you as an outlier.

The geopolitical consequences of these upgrades are profound. When Canada froze bank accounts during the trucker protests, or when PayPal and GoFundMe halted fundraising campaigns over political content, the global audience took note. These were not isolated incidents—they were *demonstrations of the fragility of financial access.* For citizens in unstable regimes, such moves confirm what many already know: if your assets exist only in official ledgers, they can disappear at the discretion of unseen actors. But for those in supposedly liberal democracies, these events puncture the illusion of financial invulnerability. Sovereignty is no longer merely a question of national independence—it is a question of *personal infrastructure.*

Technology, of course, cuts both ways. The same networks that enable surveillance also allow for sovereignty—*if used correctly.* Decentralised finance (DeFi), multisignature wallets, cold storage, and encrypted communications all offer partial remedies. But they are not foolproof, and they demand a level of intentionality that few are trained to exercise. A private key offers no recourse if lost. A self-custodied wallet offers no insurance if hacked. The difference is that control comes with responsibility. *Digital sovereignty is not free—it is earned* through education, vigilance, and structural design.

What makes today's threat landscape so challenging is not its novelty, but its subtlety. In the past, a tyrant would seize your land or plunder your vault. Today, a system might simply *deny your login credentials*. The old threats wore uniforms; the new ones wear UX design. The function is the same—the deprivation of economic agency—but the means have become abstract, efficient, and often invisible.

That is why historical awareness is essential. Because what looks like progress—cashless societies, real-time payments, centralised ID verification—can also function as regressions in autonomy. They enable new capabilities, but also new dependencies. Just as physical infrastructure shaped 20th-century geopolitics, *digital infrastructure will define 21st-century sovereignty*. And unless individuals begin to architect their own systems of redundancy, privacy, and control, they risk being programmed into obsolescence.

This is not about technophobia. It is about *technorealism*. Just as past civilisations had to navigate shifting dynamics of power—be it feudal land contracts, monarchic tax regimes, or colonial currency manipulations—today's citizen must reckon with programmable policy embedded in software. History has not ended. It has simply migrated.

And so the threats do not repeat. They *upgrade*. The tools are different, but the logic remains. Control of money is control of people. And until our systems are redesigned with human agency as the priority—not convenience or compliance—then digital elegance will merely mask institutional coercion. The only antidote is awareness, preparation, and architectural independence.

To protect wealth in the modern world is not to resist change. It is to *anticipate its trajectory*—and to build systems of ownership that can outlast not just inflation or taxation, but *intervention by design.*

Chapter 4
Redefining Wealth in a Collapsing World

What if the conventional understanding of wealth is built on a flawed foundation? Not merely because of inflation nibbling at value, taxation extracting its share, or theft undermining stability—but because the very assumptions we tether ourselves to—ownership, liquidity, convertibility, access—are becoming increasingly disconnected from the realities of how modern systems function. The neat figures on your bank statement, the title deed to your home, the tidy rows of your investment portfolio—they offer a comforting picture. But comfort, here, is not the same as control. It is a conditional benefit, granted by frameworks that reserve the right to retract or redefine that wealth—often without prior notice, and almost always without recourse.

This chapter does not open with graphs, trend lines, or economic theorems. It opens with disorientation—a deliberate unseating of assumptions. If the chapters before have illuminated the fragility of ownership and the fleeting nature of access, then what follows is the work of reconstruction. We're not here to tinker with your allocation strategy. We're here to reimagine wealth at its roots—to build a conceptual model robust enough to withstand the slow-motion unraveling of legacy finance.

At the centre of this reimagining lies an uncomfortable but clarifying insight: one can own an asset without controlling it, and one can control an asset without technically owning it. And one can lose either, without so much as a notification. In an increasingly centralised world—governed by compliance-driven intermediaries, fluid legal definitions, and ever-shifting terms of use—access is rarely absolute. It's provisional, discretionary, and often hidden behind a façade of seamless convenience. The sleeker the surface, the more opaque the machinery behind it.

Consider the self-styled sovereign individual, storing their cryptocurrency on a popular exchange. The ideology is freedom; the reality, less so—until withdrawals are frozen for "market safety" or "regulatory review." Or the homeowner who discovers, to their dismay, that their land rights bend under the weight of new zoning laws, confiscatory tax policy, or a shifting political agenda. These aren't footnotes to the system. These are baked-in features. True control, then, is not found in paperwork or platform promises. It is the ability to convert value into freedom—on your terms.

Which brings us to a necessary redefinition: in a world where old certainties fray, wealth must be reframed not as a static tally, but as an active capacity. Traditional metrics—net worth, annual yield, asset diversity—are relics of a system predicated on continuity and trust. Increasingly, the meaningful metric is not what you hold, but what you can *use* when the music stops. Can your capital move with you across borders? Can it serve you under surveillance? Can it preserve your dignity when institutions falter?

This is where the idea of *sovereign capital* emerges—a form of wealth not anchored to ledgers but to human attributes: adaptability, competence, reputation, mobility, access to decentralised knowledge networks. These are not poetic ideals. They are, in many cases, the deciding factors in whether someone weathers a storm—or is swept away by it. When economies disintegrate, it is not the most credentialed or the most capitalised who thrive—it is those with transferable skill, relational depth, and unmediated utility.

The historical record offers a hard but instructive confirmation. Jewish families fleeing pre-war Germany often survived not because of what they carried, but because of whom they knew, what they spoke, and how early they acted. Entrepreneurs in Venezuela and Zimbabwe discovered that bank accounts and bonds were poor shelter—but decentralised tools, parallel markets, and mutual trust networks often proved life-saving. Even now, in parts of Eastern Europe and South Asia, those with strategic mobility and antifragile income sources are outperforming peers tied to collapsing frameworks.

This is the beginning of a new template—a shift from financial optimisation to structural durability. Anti-fragile wealth does not resist shocks; it metabolises them. It becomes stronger through them. This demands that we discard the illusion of single-point dependability: one currency, one jurisdiction, one platform. Instead, we adopt a layered, plural strategy—where physical assets, decentralised financial tools, legal insulation, and informal social capital combine into something sturdier than the sum of its parts.

But anti-fragility is not synonymous with paranoia. It is discipline, systemisation, and choice. It's the conscious decision to hold some value in offline, untraceable formats—perhaps literally, in the form of gold or hard assets; perhaps metaphorically, in the form of memorised seed phrases, international custodial trusts, or cash-flow mechanisms that bypass geographic and political boundaries. It also includes the invisible forms of capital: your mental acuity, your health, your reputation, your right to cross a border without suspicion.

In post-default Argentina, where state currency failed and trust in institutions collapsed, people reverted to what they could trust—each other. Local scrips, barter coupons, and unregistered skills became the basis of a new economy. Doctors, mechanics, teachers—those whose contributions didn't rely on formal structures—became indispensable. This isn't some romantic footnote; it's a repeatable pattern. We've seen it in Greece, in Lebanon, in Russia—and now it echoes, uneasily, in wealthier nations grappling with inflation, censorship, and overreach.

The point isn't that fiat is dead or that cryptocurrency is a cure-all. It's that the future of wealth won't be dominated by any single model. Instead, it will be a mosaic—a patchwork of imperfect options, none of them complete, all of them conditional. Fiat currencies will still serve—but selectively. Real estate may remain valuable—but only in countries with rule of law. Digital assets will empower—but only if custody remains sovereign. The person who constructs optionality across domains—legal, digital, physical, relational—will not only endure chaos, but navigate through it with leverage.

So, this chapter won't hand you a list of "top five crisis-proof assets." That would be missing the point. Instead, we will dismantle and reconstruct your mental map. We'll challenge the comforting myth that a diversified spreadsheet equals security. We'll explore the difference between what's liquid and what's accessible. And we'll make the case that your most important safe is neither on a shelf nor on a server—it's in your ability to make decisions free from coercion, inertia, or fear.

Because collapse, when it comes, does not announce itself politely. It leaks, erodes, accumulates. But it also opens a window—for those with clarity. The old definitions of wealth won't hold. What will is your ability to adapt them. To embody your value, not just measure it. To move your wealth—not just across borders, but across paradigms. The vault is not out there. It is you. Let's start designing it.

Liquid, Private, Uncorrelated

There is a sobering truth that most portfolio theory never confronts: *your wealth is only as real as your ability to access, protect, and adapt it under duress.* In the abstract, spreadsheets and brokerage dashboards promise a neat vision of wealth allocation. But real-world disruptions—be they political, technological, or systemic—don't respect spreadsheet assumptions. In such environments, wealth ceases to be defined by its nominal size and begins to be measured by three far more consequential attributes: *liquidity, privacy,* and *non-correlation.* These are not just tactical preferences. They are structural imperatives in a world increasingly hostile to autonomy.

Each of these pillars addresses a distinct vulnerability in the architecture of modern wealth. Liquidity ensures that you can deploy value when time is scarce. Privacy protects your financial movements from exposure, seizure, or social and institutional coercion. Non-correlation shields your portfolio from cascading systemic failures. Taken together, these qualities don't just make wealth more durable—they make it *less obedient,* less legible to centralised forces, and more aligned with personal sovereignty.

Let us begin with liquidity—not the theoretical kind found in market reports, but functional, *crisis-grade* liquidity. In practical terms, liquidity is the ability to convert an asset into usable purchasing power *quickly and without penalty*. Many assets that appear "liquid" in stable markets become frozen in volatile ones. Real estate, for example, can be illiquid for months or years when buyers vanish or capital controls emerge. Even equities, despite their reputation for high tradability, can become inaccessible when brokerage platforms are throttled or regulatory freezes take effect. We witnessed this with the 2020 pandemic panic, where margin calls cascaded and trading halts paralysed platforms like Robinhood.

True liquidity, then, means more than the theoretical ability to sell. It means *control over timing, jurisdiction, and transaction*. Gold coins held physically, Bitcoin in cold storage, or even strategic cash reserves in hard currencies all satisfy this requirement to varying degrees—*not because they're perfect stores of value*, but because they preserve optionality in moments when other systems seize up.

Privacy, the second pillar, is often misunderstood as a luxury rather than a safeguard. Yet history and contemporary policy alike reveal that *visibility is vulnerability*. From China's social credit system to Western financial surveillance under the guise of "anti-money laundering" and "counter-terrorism", the ability to monitor and freeze individual assets has become frictionless. Privacy is not about evasion—it is about *discretionary visibility*. It allows one to control the exposure of financial behaviour to third parties: governments, corporations, or even vindictive individuals.

Consider the European Union's 2022 decision to restrict anonymous crypto wallets, or the United States' extensive use of Suspicious Activity Reports (SARs) by financial institutions, often without the knowledge of the person being surveilled. Or, look further back to the 1933 Executive Order 6102 in the U.S., which required citizens to surrender gold holdings under threat of imprisonment. Every one of these measures was *enabled by visibility*. The assets that could be seen could be taken. The assets that were invisible, decentralised, or deliberately obscured, often endured.

Thus, privacy is not incidental to resilient wealth. It is central. It underwrites the freedom to transact outside systems that presume the right to intervene. The best privacy strategies today involve layered defence: unhosted wallets, decentralised protocols, non-KYC exchanges, second passports, multi-jurisdictional holdings. This is not paranoia. It is *recognition that financial safety in the modern world is inversely proportional to financial visibility.*

Finally, non-correlation—the most subtle and perhaps the most misunderstood. Diversification is not sufficient if assets are all tethered to the same systemic assumptions. Holding a mix of tech stocks, real estate investment trusts, and government bonds is not diversification if all of them crash under the same macroeconomic regime. True resilience comes from holding *assets whose risk factors do not converge.* That means holding things that do not move together, and more importantly, do not *depend* on the same infrastructure.

Bitcoin, for instance, has been lauded as "digital gold", yet often behaves like a tech stock in times of market stress—exposing investors to simultaneous drawdowns. Gold, though historically uncorrelated, may suffer from transportation, storage, and confiscation risks. Real estate is both visible and jurisdiction-bound. Therefore, a robust portfolio includes *orthogonal strategies*: assets with different geographic, technological, and institutional exposures.

This includes not only asset class diversification, but *platform diversification.* If all your assets are housed within Western banking institutions, then regardless of asset class, your exposure is systemically correlated. Consider, by contrast, a person who holds: Bitcoin in self-custody, physical silver in multiple countries, farmland titled under separate trusts, and income streams from decentralised platforms. Their wealth is not simply diversified—it is *resilient across legal and technological domains.*

But these three pillars—liquidity, privacy, and non-correlation—are not merely tactical checkboxes. They represent a philosophical shift. They invite us to ask: What do we really own? What can we really move? What can we really protect? And at what point does visible wealth become a liability rather than an asset?

Throughout this book, we have examined how modern finance trades substance for symbolism. You "own" your bank balance, until it's frozen. You "own" your pension, until the currency collapses. You "own" your stock portfolio, until trading is halted. The conventional view of wealth assumes *system stability*. These three principles—*liquid, private, uncorrelated*—are designed for when that stability fails.

They are also a check on hubris. Too many financial advisors, armed with elegant models and historical averages, scoff at such ideas as fringe or overly defensive. But these models, rooted in the last fifty years of relative stability, lack predictive power in times of structural transition. Ask the citizens of Cyprus in 2013, whose deposits were confiscated under the guise of a "bail-in". Ask the Lebanese in 2019, whose banks imposed capital controls overnight. Ask Russians with frozen credit cards in 2022. Or Argentinians. Or Zimbabweans. Or any of the dozens of populations who have learned the hard way that financial models do not protect against political decisions.

To treat liquidity, privacy, and non-correlation as optional is to treat institutional trust as unconditional. That is a dangerous bet.

The goal here is not to prepare for apocalypse. It is to *design for uncertainty*. These pillars do not assume collapse—they simply recognise its possibility. And they allow for optionality even in relative stability. A well-structured life, financially and logistically, is not less effective in calm times because it is designed to endure crisis. On the contrary, it is *more effective*, because it removes dependency as a precondition for prosperity.

In summary, the pillars of liquid, private, and uncorrelated wealth do more than protect against loss—they *liberate agency*. They allow the individual to operate outside the panopticon, to store value without begging permission, to convert capital into freedom under stress.

They are the antidote to fragility—not just financial, but personal. And they form the foundation of any modern strategy for *sovereign, survivable, and self-determined* wealth.

Assets vs Access

You don't own what you can't reach. That simple principle, often overlooked in mainstream financial discourse, cuts to the heart of one of the most urgent misperceptions in modern wealth management: the conflation of *ownership* with *access*. Most people—whether retail investors, retirees, or even high-net-worth individuals—operate under the assumption that what's "in their name" is theirs. A line on a digital dashboard, a title deed, or a bank statement seems to confer real, usable control. But this assumption is fragile, and it collapses under the weight of political shocks, institutional failures, or infrastructural disruption. *What matters in crisis is not what you own in theory—but what you can actually control, retrieve, move, or utilise in practice.*

This subchapter sets out to dismantle the illusion of ownership and introduce a more robust framework for evaluating wealth in uncertain times. It does not reject the value of assets; rather, it elevates the more critical dimension: *accessibility*. The most valuable portfolio in the world means little if it's locked behind regulatory firewalls, jurisdictional bottlenecks, or technological single points of failure. And yet, our systems of wealth storage and planning rarely account for this. They remain entranced by numbers on paper, and blind to the mechanics of *retrievability under stress*.

Consider a pension fund in a country with a weakening currency and rising capital controls. The pensioner technically owns their retirement income—until the government changes the withdrawal terms, imposes a tax on foreign currency conversions, or simply delays payments indefinitely due to "fiscal constraints." At that point, ownership is legally intact, but functionally irrelevant. Or take the example of a brokerage account. The underlying equities are yours, on paper. But your ability to trade them is at the mercy of custodians, exchanges, and national policies. When trading halts occur, or platforms are geo-fenced, or margin calls are triggered by volatility, your access vanishes—even though your name remains on the asset.

Access, therefore, is not an ancillary consideration. It is the *actual expression* of ownership. And it is conditional—on infrastructure, intermediaries, jurisdiction, compliance, and stability. Most investors do not realise this until it is too late. They plan for market volatility, but not for institutional unreliability. They hedge economic risk, but not logistical or legal risk. This is not just a blind spot; it's a fundamental error in how we understand the nature of control.

Let's trace this distinction more systematically. Ownership is a legal construct. It is encoded in contracts, property rights, and institutional recognition. Access, by contrast, is *functional control.* It is the ability to deploy, move, or convert value in real time, under duress. And access exists on a spectrum. At one end are assets you physically hold and can immediately use—cash in hand, gold coins in your safe, crypto in self-custody with memorised keys. At the other end are assets you own in theory but can only access through layers of bureaucracy or trusted intermediaries—shares in custodial accounts, pensions, or even private real estate in foreign jurisdictions.

Modern finance privileges the latter. For convenience, for scalability, for integration into broader economic systems. But it comes at a cost: *dependency.* Every layer between you and your asset is a layer of vulnerability—subject to policy shifts, cyber breaches, banking outages, or worse. And during systemic stress, those layers can collapse quickly.

Take Cyprus in 2013. Overnight, depositors found that a percentage of their "guaranteed" savings were seized as part of a bank rescue package. The technical ownership remained—on paper—but access was truncated, arbitrarily. Or Argentina, where savings in U.S. dollars were forcibly converted to pesos, then subjected to withdrawal limits. In both cases, citizens held the same nominal claims they always had. But their access had been redefined by fiat.

Cryptocurrencies, particularly Bitcoin, emerged in part as a response to this structural problem. They offer a model of *non-custodial access*—where control resides directly with the individual, unmediated by institutions. But even here, the details matter. Holding Bitcoin on an exchange, or through a custodial wallet, reintroduces the same vulnerabilities. The asset may be decentralised, but your *access* is centralised. True functional control requires not just technical ownership, but *operational sovereignty*: self-custody, knowledge of recovery procedures, and resilience to censorship.

This raises a broader philosophical point. If access is the true expression of ownership, then our financial planning must shift from accumulation to configuration. Not "how much do I own?" but "what can I access, how quickly, under what conditions?" This is a radically different way to think about wealth. It forces us to look beyond asset classes and focus instead on *asset architectures*—the systems, locations, formats, and jurisdictions in which wealth is held.

A high-net-worth individual with £10 million in equities, all held through a single UK brokerage, has less resilience than someone with £2 million diversified across self-custodied crypto, offshore physical gold, multi-jurisdictional trusts, and income-generating real estate. Not because the latter has more capital, but because they have *more control across contexts*. This is not theoretical. In crisis scenarios, time is short, access is patchy, and permissions are scarce. Those who have thought through *access pathways* survive intact. Those who haven't, don't.

Access planning also invites ethical reflection. When financial systems freeze accounts, delay withdrawals, or censor transactions, they often do so under the banner of regulation, safety, or "public interest." But this reveals another layer of truth: *access is political.* It is not just a logistical or technical issue. It is a matter of who decides what you are allowed to do with your own capital—and under what narrative. That power, once granted to centralised actors, tends to expand. And rarely does it recede without disruption.

This is not a call for paranoia. It is a call for precision. Ownership is an insufficient metric of wealth resilience. Access is the missing dimension—and without it, everything else is symbolic. We must begin to ask harder questions of our wealth structures. What are the access terms? Who can override them? How quickly can I move, convert, or liquidate? Under what scenarios would access be delayed, denied, or surveilled?

For professionals, this may involve revisiting wealth storage strategies, diversifying not only across asset classes but across custodians, jurisdictions, and infrastructure types. For everyday investors, it may mean reducing exposure to digital-only platforms, understanding the risks of custodial solutions, or holding a portion of their savings in tangible, decentralised forms. For families and intergenerational planners, it may require building knowledge transmission structures so that successors can *actually access* what they inherit.

And for all of us, it means discarding the illusion that a line on a screen is equivalent to control. *It's not.* Until you can touch it, move it, or spend it without asking permission, your wealth is a promise—not a fact.

The future belongs to those who can navigate constraints—not just accumulate assets. That navigation depends on access: fast, unmediated, and sovereign. In a world where institutions are both more powerful and more brittle, this is no longer optional. It is the difference between security and theatre, between symbolic wealth and real capital. And it is the foundation upon which any truly antifragile wealth strategy must rest.

Sovereign Capital: You Are the Vault

The most overlooked asset class in modern finance is the human being. Not their labour, not their productivity, not their credit score—*but their sovereignty.* The prevailing financial models fixate on external assets: stocks, bonds, property, metals, currencies. These are stored in vaults, accounts, registries, or protocols. Yet history, crisis after crisis, proves an inconvenient truth: **what survives systemic failure is not what you store, but *who you become.***

This subchapter examines a radical but enduring idea—*that the ultimate vault is not a bank, a blockchain, or a private trust—it is you.* When access to wealth is impaired, when institutions collapse or reconstitute under hostile terms, the only consistently recoverable capital is the knowledge, resilience, adaptability, and sovereignty embedded within the individual. *You are the infrastructure.*

This is not a motivational platitude. It's a survival principle.

Let's begin by observing the discrepancy between technical wealth and functional survival. A person who owns a diversified portfolio of digital and physical assets—say, equities, real estate, crypto, and offshore bullion—may appear financially insulated. But if they lack the ability to manage, move, secure, or transform those assets under emergent conditions—across borders, jurisdictions, systems, or timeframes—their "wealth" is theoretical. In contrast, someone with fewer tangible assets but deep operational knowledge, multilingual fluency, crisis literacy, portable skills, and cross-jurisdictional insight can often *reconstruct* wealth faster and more securely from first principles.

We see this in post-collapse environments across history. In post-Soviet Eastern Europe, for example, it wasn't the bureaucrats or industrialists who navigated the vacuum most effectively—it was those who understood arbitrage, cross-border movement, interpersonal trust-building, and parallel economic logic. During Argentina's periodic crises, or Venezuela's collapse, or Lebanon's currency implosion, the pattern repeats: the most valuable "asset" is not what's in storage—it's the ability to read change early, act decisively, relocate mentally and physically, and establish continuity through ambiguity.

The financial industry has no asset class for this. And yet it is the *only* form of wealth that is invulnerable to third-party seizure, denial of service, court orders, inflation, capital controls, or hardware failure. This is not about rejecting external assets; it is about recognising that **assets are not sovereign—people are**. And those who understand this build systems that revolve around personal agency, not passive dependency.

What does it mean to treat yourself as the vault?

At the surface level, it means reclaiming *custody* of your knowledge. Not outsourcing critical skills to advisors, apps, or platforms without understanding how they operate. Not assuming your accountant will know how to navigate a seizure. Not presuming your exchange or wallet provider will honour withdrawals during systemic stress. In sovereign capital theory, *your understanding is your insurance.*

Go deeper. Being the vault also means decentralising your competencies. Are you dependent on a single skillset or job market for survival? Can you earn, transact, and store value across multiple platforms and geographies? Are you building layers of optionality, or are you optimising for convenience? Sovereign capital thrives on *redundancy, modularity, and self-reliance.* This is not about doomsday prepping—it is about designing a life that does not collapse when a single institution does.

Then there is the psychological layer: *emotional antifragility.* Many people freeze, defer, or comply when the system shifts beneath their feet—not because they are weak, but because they were conditioned to associate security with conformity. Sovereign individuals internalise a different posture. They assume that disruption is normal, and that institutions will always, eventually, act in their own interest—often at the expense of those they claim to protect. This realism is not paranoia; it is precision. It liberates the individual from illusion and empowers decisive, independent action.

There's also the epistemic component: *how you build your worldview.* Are your ideas inherited, or interrogated? Are you following mainstream financial advice that only works in stable conditions? Are you trained to distinguish between short-term volatility and long-term regime change? Sovereign capital doesn't just act differently—it *thinks* differently. It does not outsource intellectual authority to legacy institutions or cultural norms. It questions, tests, and reconfigures.

Practical applications of this mindset are abundant, but often overlooked.

A globally mobile professional who learns how to use privacy-preserving payment protocols, self-custody crypto, legal entity structures across borders, and real-world peer-to-peer trade networks is far more insulated from shocks than a passive investor with a traditional portfolio in a high-trust jurisdiction. Why? Because they *can pivot.* They can transfer, repurpose, relocalise, and rebuild faster. They are their own continuity plan.

A mother who trains herself in decentralised education, direct community barter, and emergency provisioning is acting as a sovereign wealth system for her family. She is not waiting for the state, the school, or the financial system to recover. She *is the system.* And that's the core insight here: *resilience is internal, not institutional.*

This principle was well understood in traditional societies. The oral transmission of trade knowledge, kinship networks of reciprocity, and embedded social capital ensured that value persisted even when regimes fell. In the modern world, we've abstracted and professionalised this wisdom into silos—finance, law, compliance, logistics—but we've lost the unifying insight: *human adaptability is the original vault structure.* Everything else is a layer on top.

Importantly, this shift in perspective also reframes the purpose of external assets. Under sovereign capital theory, assets are not endpoints; they are *tools*. They are valuable not because they sit in your portfolio, but because they serve your agency. If they compromise that agency—by being illiquid, surveilled, centralised, or jurisdictionally constrained—they are *liabilities in disguise.* A vault that can be opened by someone else is not a vault. A "secure" investment that you can't liquidate without asking permission is not security.

This leads us to a powerful reframing: *wealth is not measured in holdings—it is measured in optionality.* Sovereign capital builds optionality across dimensions: geographical, legal, digital, interpersonal, cognitive. This is what protects you when the grid flickers, when trust collapses, when capital controls are imposed, or when markets misprice everything.

Think of this as a portfolio of capacities:

Mobility: Can you leave when it's time to go—and arrive somewhere prepared?

Memory: Do you know how your systems work—or are you dependent on institutions to remind you?

Modularity: Can your wealth systems shrink, adapt, or scale based on context?

Discretion: Can you act without broadcasting your intentions or needing consensus?

These aren't technical traits. They're learned disciplines. And they compound. A sovereign individual is not someone who owns nothing; it is someone whose capital is not hostage to any single point of failure. They can live in the world, transact in it, thrive within its borders—but *never depend on them absolutely*.

Sovereign capital is not a rejection of community, cooperation, or society. It's the foundation that allows for *voluntary interdependence*, not coerced dependence. It's the difference between a citizen and a subject. Between someone who stores their life in a bank and someone who carries their life in their blood, their memory, their skill.

The sovereign vault is not a physical space. It is a set of choices. To learn, not delegate. To observe systems soberly. To practice exit, not just voice. To build for contingency, not continuity. And most importantly, to design wealth that aligns with agency, not just arithmetic.

When you become the vault, no one can seize your core capital. Not a government, not a hacker, not a crash. They can take your assets—but not your adaptability. They can deny your access—but not your comprehension. They can rewrite the rules—but not your playbook.

In a collapsing world, *you are the infrastructure.* Build accordingly.

Anti-Fragile Wealth Systems: Structures That Gain from Disorder

When most people think of wealth, they imagine a delicate balance: a portfolio carefully structured, calibrated to resist volatility, to withstand recessions, to survive downturns. *But survival is not the standard.* Resilience, by definition, endures shocks. Yet *anti-fragility*—a term popularised by Nassim Nicholas Taleb—goes further: it thrives on chaos. It improves under pressure. It evolves with disruption. And in a world increasingly defined by instability—whether monetary, geopolitical, environmental, or institutional—only wealth systems that internalise this principle will endure with strength, not fragility.

This subchapter seeks to redefine wealth architecture: not merely as a hedge against collapse, but as a system designed to *absorb disorder and convert it into advantage*. We explore what makes an asset structure anti-fragile, examine historical and contemporary examples, and analyse how thoughtful individuals and families can redesign their wealth ecosystems to not just survive crisis—but improve because of it.

To begin, we must distinguish three conceptual categories:

Fragile systems break under stress. A savings account denominated in a collapsing fiat currency. A business with one revenue stream tied to one political jurisdiction. A retirement plan reliant on government promises.

Resilient systems endure stress without transformation. Gold bars stored securely. A diversified index fund. A hard asset with low leverage.

Anti-fragile systems *benefit* from stress. These systems have asymmetric upside in volatile environments. They are adaptive, decentralised, often redundant, and difficult to suppress.

The goal, therefore, is to engineer a *portfolio of asymmetries*—systems that lose little when wrong but gain massively when right. This applies to financial instruments, legal entities, human capital, and social networks. Let's examine each in turn.

1. Anti-Fragile Instruments

The most classically cited example of anti-fragility is the **out-of-the-money option**. It bleeds value in still waters but becomes explosively valuable in a shock event. During the 2008 financial crisis, traders who had structured portfolios around volatility gained massively. But options are not the only instruments that express anti-fragile characteristics. Consider:

Bitcoin and censorship-resistant assets: Whatever one's view on crypto fundamentals, decentralised assets gain relevance—and often value—during monetary repression, banking crises, or currency devaluations. They are not resistant to volatility; they *feed on it.* Their very justification is fragility elsewhere.

Uncorrelated assets in distressed environments: Certain agricultural commodities, water rights, and timberland have shown to not just hold value in downturns, but to *perform counter-cyclically*, especially when global systems misprice risk.

Cash-like equivalents in declining jurisdictions: USD-denominated assets, when held offshore or in stable jurisdictions, can yield enormous gains purely from capital flight effects when local currencies collapse.

The key insight? Fragility in mainstream systems is a precondition for asymmetric gains in niche or emergent ones.

2. Structural Anti-Fragility

Beyond asset selection, there is the structure in which wealth is held—often more determinative of survival than the asset itself. For instance:

Jurisdictional diversification is anti-fragile. Holding assets, citizenships, or legal entities across countries not only protects from localised risk—it allows one to capitalise on capital controls, taxation shifts, or monetary experiments by being agile. It is not just a defensive posture—it opens offensive opportunities.

Layered ownership structures can create asymmetric legal advantages. Trusts, foundations, or DAOs (decentralised autonomous organisations) are not merely tax vehicles; they're architectural tools for absorbing regulatory change while maintaining functional control.

Decentralised physical custody—such as bullion in private vaults in multiple countries, or secure multi-signature wallets for crypto—creates friction against seizure, but also optionality in routing access across different legal and logistical environments.

In a fragile world, the structure matters more than the content.

3. The Anti-Fragile Human

Anti-fragile wealth systems are impossible to build without anti-fragile individuals. That is not philosophy—it's engineering.

The ability to adapt, pivot, and reallocate rapidly is not merely a function of portfolio design. It stems from *cognitive flexibility*, *emotional sobriety*, and *strategic literacy*. Consider:

A skilled tradesperson or technical operator can rebuild value in any economy. Their skills are mobile and liquid in a way stocks are not.

A person fluent in multiple legal and financial systems, who understands risk signals and can interpret institutional failure early, has an edge that no broker can replicate.

An individual with a wide and trustworthy network of global contacts—entrepreneurs, operators, problem-solvers—is anti-fragile by virtue of what economists call *relational capital.* This asset class cannot be confiscated.

In chaotic environments, *a sovereign individual is worth more than a passive investor.*

4. Dynamic Liquidity and Optionality

Anti-fragile systems are rarely static. They're built on optionality—the power to change course without penalty. This is why access matters more than ownership. A trust that lets you move capital between jurisdictions discreetly is more powerful than outright ownership of a property that cannot be liquidated during capital controls.

Liquidity is misunderstood. It's not just about asset convertibility. It's about *mobility under constraint.* An apartment in an authoritarian regime with rent controls and frozen FX markets may be technically valuable—but practically useless. In contrast, a diversified stash of privacy coins or bearer instruments can be worthless in calm times, but priceless when capital controls hit.

Liquidity under pressure is the true test of antifragility.

5. Self-Sustaining Loops and Anti-Fragile Ecosystems

Wealth systems that *produce* their own security and feedback improve over time. These include:

Productive land with community governance: Agro-ecological land that produces food, medicine, and community barter during supply chain collapse gains value in stress.

Peer-to-peer economic systems: Platforms that connect freelancers, suppliers, and clients outside centralised systems become more valuable as institutions falter.

Family offices or private networks that integrate legal, operational, and educational tools: These are meta-assets. They not only protect value—they *generate knowledge* that compounds.

When your wealth system feeds your learning loop, it becomes self-reinforcing.

Why Most "Diversified" Portfolios Fail the Fragility Test

Traditional portfolios may appear diversified, but they are often systemically correlated. Equities, bonds, and real estate all depend on functioning markets, legal continuity, and fiat credibility. When those fail together—as they did during the Great Depression, the GFC, and in Venezuela—their correlation spikes to 1.

What appears as diversification in spreadsheets is often *concentration in systemic trust.*

An anti-fragile portfolio instead diversifies across systems: fiat and non-fiat, regulated and permissionless, tangible and digital, domestic and foreign, short and long duration, transparent and discreet. This is not simply a strategy. It is a worldview. It assumes *the system is the risk*, and designs accordingly.

Anti-Fragility is Not Maximalism. It Is Modularity.

Crucially, anti-fragile wealth systems are not maximalist. They do not put everything into crypto, or gold, or land. They build *modular ecosystems*—each module fails safely and independently.

This architecture borrows from engineering, where systems with high uptime—aircraft, satellites, nuclear facilities—are built with *redundancy and graceful failure.* The same must apply to our wealth. A failed bank should not crash your liquidity. A frozen jurisdiction should not erase your access. A seized account should not devastate your plan.

Each failure mode becomes *a stress test*—and a trigger for strategic upgrade.

Final Insight

The age of passive wealth is ending. The assumption that long-term equity markets will deliver, that pensions will honour their terms, that inflation is transitory, or that jurisdictions will remain investor-friendly—all these are faith-based premises dressed up as financial planning.

Anti-fragile wealth systems ask a deeper, braver question: *What if none of it comes back?* And they answer with a model that does not merely survive collapse—it *extracts energy from it.*

If you build your assets like a machine that improves under heat, adapts under threat, and compounds under pressure, then you are not just wealthy. You are sovereign.

And sovereignty, in a fragile world, *is the rarest form of capital.*

Chapter 5
Currencies of the Future (and Past)

Money, for all its shine and structure, has never truly been what it claims to be. Beneath the polished sheen of financial dashboards, beneath the proclamations of central bankers and the abstractions of modern economics, there lies something far more ancient—and arguably, far more human: a web of trust, shared belief, and collective narrative. Strip away the interface, and what remains is a social fiction, albeit a powerful one. Every currency, no matter how technologically advanced or historically obscure, survives not through coercion, but through consensus. It lives as long as enough people believe in its story—and vanishes when they no longer do.

Still, most people—perhaps out of habit, or faith in continuity—cling to a single monetary lens. One unit of measurement. One numerical yardstick by which all value is judged. This intellectual monism is more than just limited—it's perilous. When the dominant financial infrastructure falters, as history assures us it eventually will, those confined to single-currency thinking are often left unmoored. Their labour, their talents, even their assets—everything they've built—can feel suddenly mispriced, even meaningless. They possess money, yes. But value? That slips through their fingers.

This chapter is a confrontation with that kind of blindness. It's an invitation—no, a challenge—to step outside the rigid mental architecture built by centralised monetary systems and consider something broader. Richer. More real. We turn our gaze toward currencies that have existed on the periphery—born in crisis, sustained in shadow, and often more durable than their official counterparts. These alternatives don't wait for permission. They simply emerge, and persist, because people must eat, trade, and trust one another—even when the scaffolding of state and system gives way.

To speak of the future of money, we must begin by abandoning the idea that it wears only one face. It doesn't. It never has.

Barter, Reputation, and the Quiet Authority of Favours

Wherever societies falter—be it through hyperinflation, war, or bureaucratic collapse—the official currency tends to be among the first institutions to lose its grip. What comes next is rarely sleek or efficient, but it is always responsive. When the state's promise becomes hollow, people revert to fundamentals: What do you need? What can I offer? Are you someone I can count on?

In Zimbabwe, as its currency spiralled into irrelevance, fuel was exchanged for seed, and bread for labour. The rouble still had printed authority in the twilight of the Soviet Union, but the *blat* system—a web of informal connections, favours, and barter—was what actually moved goods and opened doors. During the depths of the Greek debt crisis, entire micro-economies bloomed through Local Exchange Trading Systems (LETS), where services were traded without a euro in sight: a dental filling might be paid for with firewood, vegetables, or help with a home repair.

These aren't quaint tales from the outskirts of history. They are signals. Proof points. They tell us what value does when its traditional vessel is punctured. Time and again, communities have constructed resilient forms of exchange from trust and proximity, not legal tender. The neighbour who turns up when needed becomes more valuable than a high-yield savings account you can't access. Reliability begins to matter more than receivables.

And perhaps we shouldn't be surprised. These systems are not temporary aberrations. They are expressions of something deeper and older than coin or credit: the human urge to exchange, to reciprocate, to collaborate based on shared context and mutual need. Money, in this light, is not the origin of trade—it is its abstraction. Before there were banks, there was barter. Before there were ledgers, there was reputation.

So when we ask what happens to currency in crisis, we're really grappling with a more foundational question: How do people continue to coordinate, reward, and sustain each other when the tools of the state stop functioning? What survives when the plug is pulled?

And, to be plain about it—what still holds value when the power goes out?

Gold, Silver, and Timeless Metals

While barter and favour may be the default in collapse, metals have always served as a bridge between worlds. *Portable, durable, divisible, and scarce*, precious metals are the oldest form of money still in use. Their strength lies not in their modern utility, but in their historical continuity. When institutions fail, people reach for what *has never failed before.*

Gold, in particular, performs not because it yields—but because it doesn't decay. It is a bet not on growth, but on *survival.* Across empires and centuries, it has served as a ledger that does not erase. Whether used by Roman emperors, Ottoman merchants, or World War II refugees sewing coins into coats, gold is the last refuge when belief collapses.

But it's also important not to over-romanticise metals. They are not magical. They don't grow. They can be seized, regulated, or rendered temporarily illiquid. What they offer is not perfection, but *finality.* In an over-leveraged, digitally mediated economy, the appeal of something *that settles without counterparties* is profound.

Silver, too, has historical importance—not as a vault asset, but as a transactional one. In many post-collapse environments, silver coinage retained local value far longer than fiat. It was divisible, portable, and known. And in certain black markets, it still serves that role today.

To treat metals as relics is to ignore their function in systemic resets. *They are not outdated—they are uncorrelated.* They represent a form of value immune to policymaking, narrative manipulation, or digital revocation.

Building a Poly-Currency Mindset

If there is one practical insight that flows from this chapter, it is this: *Stop thinking in single units.* Wealth today is multi-dimensional. Value moves through multiple rails—legal, digital, informal, and interpersonal. To survive and thrive, you must become fluent across them.

A "poly-currency mindset" is not a portfolio allocation. It is a cognitive posture. It means understanding:

That **state-backed currency** is just one lens of value, and not always the most durable.

That **social capital**—trust, reciprocity, and reputation—can function as currency when money breaks.

That **metals, barter goods, skills, favours, and time** may serve as currencies depending on context.

That **crypto-assets and decentralised protocols**, while volatile, are attempting to build new layers of permissionless exchange.

That **geographic and legal arbitrage**—the ability to operate in multiple monetary systems—can itself be a currency.

It also means rethinking storage. Not just where you keep value, but *how* it is stored. In collapse, access matters more than ownership. A skill you can trade is better than a certificate you cannot redeem. A useful network is better than a pension that has been politically repurposed. A kilo of silver is better than a digital account under lockdown.

This mindset does not require abandoning fiat. It simply means *not being owned by it.* It means holding wealth in forms that are harder to freeze, easier to hide, quicker to trade, and resilient in ambiguity.

The Future is Not a Replacement. It is a Layering.

A mistake often made in both libertarian and technocratic circles is to assume that the future of currency lies in *replacement.* That the dollar will be toppled. That Bitcoin will become the singular global standard. Or that central bank digital currencies (CBDCs) will erase cash altogether.

Reality will be messier. The future of currency is not singular—it is *layered.* It will involve multiple overlapping systems: formal, informal, analogue, digital, regulated, grey. Some will dominate. Others will coexist. A robust strategy must *interoperate* with many.

Think of the Nigerian market trader who uses naira for taxes, dollars for savings, and airtime minutes as petty cash. Or the Venezuelan technician who trades labour for food, holds crypto for remittances, and buys gold dust from smugglers. These people are not economists—but they are masterful economic actors. They think in *systems*, not slogans.

And this, ultimately, is the lesson. The most resilient individuals do not predict the future—they *prepare for multiple ones.*

Final Thought

Currency is not merely a medium of exchange. It is an operating system for civilisation. It defines what we value, how we measure worth, and how we relate to one another under constraint. In stable societies, that system is invisible. But under stress, it reveals itself—sometimes brutally.

This chapter invites the reader to move beyond default assumptions, to build resilience not just in what they hold, but in how they *think about holding.* The future will not be centrally managed. It will be contested. And in that world, *those who speak multiple currencies will not just survive—they will lead.*

Bitcoin and the New Exodus

A currency that no state controls. A balance sheet with no counterparty. A borderless asset that you can carry across a war zone in your head, if needed. To many, this sounds like economic salvation. To others, it sounds like a mirage. Bitcoin sits at the intersection of freedom and fragility, offering a new kind of sovereignty—but only to those who understand its terms.

Since its inception in 2009, Bitcoin has been framed as many things: a hedge against inflation, a protest against monetary policy, a technological marvel, a decentralised payment network, and more recently, a store of value. But as with all tools, its meaning is shaped not by its code, but by *context.* What begins as liberation can calcify into ideology. What promises mobility can, if misunderstood, become a gilded cage. Bitcoin is not a utopia. It is *an instrument.* And whether it serves as escape or entrapment depends entirely on the user's literacy, psychology, and strategy.

This chapter examines Bitcoin as a pivotal force in modern asset protection—neither dismissing it as hype nor romanticising it as a revolution. We explore its role in financial exodus: how it enables exit from fragile currencies, from politicised institutions, and from jurisdictions hostile to capital flight. We also dissect the traps—technical, philosophical, and behavioural—that can turn a tool of empowerment into a new dependency. The goal is not to evangelise or reject, but to interrogate: *what kind of freedom does Bitcoin offer, and at what price?*

From Code to Coordinates: The Infrastructure of Exit

Historically, exodus has meant movement: physical relocation to avoid persecution, confiscation, or collapse. But in the digital age, movement can occur on another plane—*the movement of capital beyond the reach of state control.* Bitcoin enables this, not because it's anonymous (it isn't), nor because it's untraceable (it's publicly traceable forever), but because it exists outside the permission structures of traditional finance. No central bank can inflate it. No government can freeze it with a phone call to your broker. No customs officer can detect it on your person—if you've memorised a twelve-word seed phrase, your assets can travel without form.

This is more than technical novelty. It is *jurisdictional arbitrage made portable.* For those living under regimes where capital controls, asset seizures, or hyperinflation are real and present threats, Bitcoin is not a speculative game—it is *a lifeboat.* In Lebanon, Venezuela, Nigeria, Turkey, and Argentina, it has already functioned as a means of wealth escape, allowing families to bypass failing currencies, censored banks, and corrupt bureaucracies. For the politically dissident or the economically exiled, Bitcoin offers something rare: an *uncensorable exit route.*

But with this power comes risk. Bitcoin is not forgiving. It does not forget lost passwords, nor does it offer customer support. It does not reverse transactions. It is trustless, but also merciless. For all its radical potential, it demands radical responsibility.

Sovereignty Requires Skill, Not Slogans

The idea of "being your own bank" is compelling—until one considers what banks actually do. They manage security, backups, legal compliance, insurance, estate transfers, fraud detection, and recovery processes. In a sovereign crypto context, *you are now responsible for all of that.* The convenience of custodianship disappears, replaced by operational risk.

Thousands have lost their entire net worth to misplaced keys, phishing attacks, faulty hardware wallets, or simple user error. Bitcoin does not discriminate. Its neutrality is absolute—brilliant in design, brutal in application. And so the tool that promises sovereignty also demands competence. The same freedom that liberates from institutions also strips away their guardrails.

And it's not just technical skill. *Psychological readiness* is essential. Bitcoin's volatility, ideological fervour, and tribal culture can distort rational judgment. Many users, attracted by its promise of independence, end up mimicking the same behaviours that made them vulnerable in legacy systems—blind trust in charismatic figures, overexposure to a single asset, or ideological echo chambers that reject nuance.

In this sense, Bitcoin is not merely a financial instrument—it is a *mirror*. It reflects the user's maturity, mindset, and risk tolerance with ruthless precision.

The Trap of Maximalism

Bitcoin maximalism—the belief that Bitcoin is not just a tool but *the only valid tool*—is increasingly common in online discourse. This worldview rejects altcoins, fiat currencies, and sometimes even diversification itself. It is a doctrine of purity, one that mirrors religious zeal more than investment analysis.

To be clear, Bitcoin's architecture remains unparalleled in terms of decentralisation, liquidity, and security. No other crypto asset has its combination of hash rate, network effect, and institutional integration. But to elevate it from superior to *exclusive* is to abandon strategic thinking for dogma.

The risk here is not philosophical—it's practical. Maximalism can lead to over-concentration, false certainty, and dangerous blind spots. It can convince holders that their Bitcoin is unseizable (it isn't), untrackable (it isn't), or immune from regulation (it won't be). It can encourage passive holding in situations where strategic liquidation or rotation might be wiser.

Exit is not a one-time act—it is an ongoing posture. And that posture must remain adaptable, not absolutist. Bitcoin is powerful, but it is not omnipotent.

The Surveillance Arms Race

As governments catch up with crypto, new tensions emerge. Bitcoin's public ledger is both a strength and a vulnerability. Every transaction, once made, is visible forever. With the rise of blockchain analytics firms, surveillance capabilities are now industrial-scale. Chainalysis, Elliptic, and other firms provide real-time tracking services to law enforcement and financial institutions, enabling them to link wallet addresses to identities with increasing accuracy.

This means that while Bitcoin enables permissionless movement, it does not ensure *private* movement. Those who assume it offers anonymity are mistaken. Bitcoin is *pseudonymous*, not anonymous. Once your identity is linked to a wallet—via a KYC exchange, IP trace, or metadata leak—your financial behaviour becomes legible across time.

This surveillance potential makes state tolerance of Bitcoin paradoxical. On one hand, it threatens capital control. On the other, it offers an *immutable map of economic dissent.* And in authoritarian settings, that map can be weaponised.

To mitigate this, users must educate themselves about privacy practices, including the use of mixers (where legal), privacy wallets, non-KYC acquisition, and even multi-jurisdictional asset dispersion. The point is not paranoia. The point is realism: *liberation without operational discipline is not freedom—it is exposure.*

The Bitcoin Diaspora

Despite these risks, the Bitcoin ecosystem continues to evolve. It is no longer merely a currency. It is a movement, an infrastructure stack, a set of social norms, and a parallel financial system with its own rules and rails. Around the world, this network is forming what could be called a *diaspora of economic dissidents*—coders, entrepreneurs, investors, refugees, and sovereign individuals building a life outside legacy constraints.

This diaspora is not defined by borders, but by shared incentives. It spans hardware manufacturers in Prague, liquidity providers in Lagos, privacy activists in Buenos Aires, and digital nomads in Bangkok. For many, Bitcoin is not a speculative asset—it is *a passport to optionality*.

And yet, even among this group, the challenges remain. How do you pass on wealth held in cryptographic form? How do you prove solvency to institutions who don't recognise your asset? How do you access your holdings under duress? These are not merely financial questions—they are architectural. *A resilient Bitcoin strategy is not just about holding—it's about preparing.*

Conclusion Without Saying "In Conclusion"

Bitcoin is a paradox: a tool for both escape and entrapment, freedom and fragility. It offers something precious—control over one's financial destiny—but only to those willing to shoulder its responsibilities. It is not a shortcut. It is not a panacea. It is a frontier, and like all frontiers, it rewards the prepared and punishes the naive.

In a collapsing monetary landscape, Bitcoin may serve as the bridge to a post-fiat world. But it is only a bridge. True financial sovereignty lies not in holding Bitcoin alone, but in *understanding its limits, mastering its risks, and integrating it within a broader anti-fragile architecture.*

This chapter invites you to treat Bitcoin seriously—not as dogma, not as gospel, but as *strategy*. In a world of programmable trust and programmable traps, discernment becomes the highest currency of all.

Barter, Reputation, and Favour Economies

How communities reinvent value exchange under collapse

There are moments in history when money stops working—not metaphorically, but functionally. Paper notes lose trust. Banks stop opening. Credit ceases to flow. And what remains is the fundamental human need to exchange value. In such times, it is not digital apps or fiat currencies that determine survival. It is relationships. It is skills. It is memory, trust, and the ability to deliver utility directly. When the formal economy breaks down, *informal economies rise—not as a regression, but as an adaptation.*

This subchapter examines how barter, favour networks, and reputation-based systems emerge during systemic failure. Far from being chaotic or primitive, these parallel systems often exhibit remarkable coordination, moral logic, and resilience. To study them is not to look backward—it is to look *sideways*, at the latent architectures of cooperation that conventional finance conceals but crisis reveals.

Barter is often romanticised as the earliest form of trade. In reality, it is one of the most *deliberate and demanding.* Without a common medium of exchange, barter requires trust, negotiation, timing, and a tight social graph. It is not scalable, but it is *intimate.* And that intimacy becomes crucial when institutions collapse.

When Money Breaks, Memory Steps In

In Argentina's 2001 economic collapse, banks froze deposits and inflation gutted savings overnight. Almost instantly, barter clubs—known as *trueques*—sprang up across the country. At their peak, these networks involved over 6 million people. Doctors traded services for bread. Mechanics exchanged labour for clothing. Entire economies functioned without pesos. What made it possible wasn't an app or even a ledger. It was *reputation.* The community remembered who provided what, and who kept their word. Value was a function of participation and perceived reliability.

Similarly, in Greece during its debt crisis, informal food swaps, cooperative pharmacies, and non-monetary trade surged. In some cases, towns issued local currencies or credit notes to keep commerce flowing. But more often, trust itself became the currency. A farmer with eggs could trade with a neighbour who baked bread, not because they agreed on a universal price, but because they had a shared understanding of need and fairness. *It is trust, not tokens, that underwrites human economies in collapse.*

This principle holds true in less visible cases as well. In refugee camps, in prisons, in informal settlements—wherever formal money loses its authority—*people revert not to chaos, but to custom.* They negotiate norms. They enforce reputation. They build economies not from abstract value, but from concrete reciprocity.

The Reputation Ledger Is Always Running

Modern finance assumes an external ledger: a bank statement, an account balance, a transactional history. But in favour economies, the ledger is *internal*—held in the minds of participants, reinforced through social cues, and maintained by communal norms. Reputation functions as a decentralised credit score, but with far richer texture.

If you're generous when others are in need, your stock rises. If you disappear during scarcity, it drops. You cannot game this system by clever branding. You build capital through *character*—not only what you offer, but how and when you offer it.

In some cultures, this form of wealth is formalised. In Pacific Island societies, systems like *kula exchange* and *moka* operate on delayed reciprocity: elaborate gifting rituals that are less about consumption than about status, cohesion, and trust. The "currency" is not the object traded, but the *obligation it creates.* Wealth in such a system is not about accumulation, but circulation.

Contrast this with today's debt-based monetary system, where trust is institutional and fungibility is prized. The favour economy inverts that. It is based on *specific trust,* not generalised currency. It is sticky, not liquid. But in the context of collapse, that specificity becomes a strength. When institutions dissolve, your most valuable assets are *who you know, what they remember, and what they're willing to do for you.*

Crisis Accelerates Reciprocity

One of the more quietly astonishing features of post-collapse environments is how quickly people revert to cooperative instincts. The assumption that disaster breeds selfishness is mostly a myth—popularised more by Hollywood than history. Sociologist Rebecca Solnit, in her research on disasters, found that mutual aid tends to spike immediately after catastrophe. People organise food sharing, housing swaps, transport logistics, and neighbourhood security—all without formal authority or payment.

In New Orleans after Hurricane Katrina, grassroots "barter clinics" emerged when medical systems failed. In Syria's war-torn regions, bakeries operated on IOUs, prioritising families by need rather than solvency. These were not acts of charity. They were *economic adaptations* to environments where central coordination had collapsed. Such systems often outperform slow-moving aid bureaucracies.

The psychology here matters. In stable times, people guard their time and goods jealously. But in visible crisis, *the calculus changes.* Reciprocity becomes more valuable than profit, because future access to help is more important than present cash. A loaf of bread today may earn a life-saving favour tomorrow. The informal economy becomes a distributed insurance network. And *the premiums are paid in generosity, competence, and reliability.*

Technology's Double Edge

One might assume that in the digital age, informal economies would vanish. But the opposite is true: *technology has augmented their precision and reach.* Peer-to-peer apps, decentralised marketplaces, and encrypted communication channels allow informal exchanges to scale while remaining unregulated.

Consider the rise of *timebanking*, where users trade hours of service rather than currency. Platforms like TimeRepublik or local LETS

(Local Exchange Trading Systems) record the hours you give, not the money you earn. The unit of account is time itself. And while these models rarely achieve mainstream scale, they flourish in tight communities and crisis contexts—where trust and utility matter more than liquidity.

Likewise, encrypted messaging apps now serve as infrastructure for informal trade in collapsing regions. In Venezuela, barter arrangements are often coordinated via WhatsApp. In Zimbabwe, community groups use Telegram to set fair exchange rates for staples and arrange goods-for-services swaps. These are not curiosities. They are previews of *post-institutional coordination systems.*

But there is a paradox here. While technology enables decentralised barter and reputation systems, it also introduces new forms of surveillance and exploitation. The very apps that facilitate informal trade can also be weaponised by authoritarian states. The challenge is not to abandon tools, but to *understand their trade-offs.* Favour economies thrive on trust, not data extraction.

Lessons for the Wealth-Conscious Reader

For the reader thinking in terms of sovereign capital or anti-fragile systems, favour and barter economies may seem quaint. But their implications are profound. In a world of rising systemic fragility—where institutions are overstretched and currencies debased—*liquidity alone is no longer a sufficient defence.* You must also invest in *resilience*, and resilience is often social before it is financial.

Ask: who would help you if your bank account were frozen? Who would feed your children if your credit card stopped working? What value can you offer in a world where money is distrusted? The answers to these questions are not found in spreadsheets, but in your habits, your community, and your adaptability.

The most sophisticated portfolio is useless if it cannot be *accessed, translated, or trusted* when it matters. That's where favour economies offer insight. They show that value exchange is more than numbers—it is *narrative*, *reputation*, and *trust.* These are assets that cannot be taxed, seized, or inflated. But they must be cultivated continuously.

To that end, one might consider building not just wealth, but *economic relationships*. Trading your time, your skills, your knowledge—outside conventional systems—strengthens both you and your network. It signals reliability. It earns you trust equity. And when crisis comes, it is often those with *social liquidity*, not just monetary liquidity, who endure best.

Final Insight

In times of collapse, people do not wait for instructions. They *improvise economies*. They repurpose trust. They trade in what is remembered, not in what is printed. In that context, barter, reputation, and favour are not relics of a pre-monetary past—they are the scaffolding of future viability.

Understanding this is not a call to abandon money, but to recognise its limits. A resilient strategy must account not only for asset classes, but for *human classes*—the network of individuals who know your name, value your presence, and remember what you gave when it was hardest to give.

In a collapsing world, *those relationships may become your most spendable form of capital.*

Gold, Silver, and Timeless Metals

Why the oldest forms of money still have a place in the future of wealth resilience

It is often said that gold has no yield. That it sits idle, producing neither interest nor innovation. But to reduce precious metals to passive relics is to miss the point entirely. *Gold is not a growth asset—it is an integrity asset.* It is what remains when systems built on trust fail. It is what endures when abstractions like currency, credit, and consensus no longer hold. And more than that, it is a mirror: of how civilisations understand value, permanence, and risk.

To dismiss gold and silver as obsolete is to commit the same error every collapsing regime has made: assuming that institutional stability is permanent, and that monetary architecture is immune to entropy. But time has repeatedly proven otherwise. Precious metals remain valuable not despite their ancient pedigree, but *because of it.* Their relevance is not metaphysical. It is practical, empirical, and historically consistent.

The Architecture of Tangible Trust

Unlike digital currencies, precious metals are not dependent on grid infrastructure, internet access, or the functioning of a centralised ledger. They are *off-network*, *non-permissioned*, and *recognised globally.* They are among the few assets that require no third-party validation to retain their worth. A gold coin does not ask who minted it. Its weight and purity *are* the proof. In a context where custodians may become adversaries and systems may freeze, this is not an aesthetic detail—it is a structural advantage.

Silver, often overshadowed by gold in financial commentary, offers an even more granular use case. While gold is suited to wealth preservation in bulk, silver functions as a practical medium of exchange during disruption. It is divisible, portable, and psychologically intuitive. Historically, it has served as small-scale money where fiat collapsed, from Weimar Germany to 1990s Argentina. And unlike luxury assets or rare collectibles, silver remains sufficiently abundant to facilitate broad-based trade. *It is not just a store of value—it is a tool of continuity.*

The Historical Record: Not Just Nostalgia

Every major currency collapse of the past century has validated the enduring role of precious metals. In Zimbabwe, as the local dollar spiralled into oblivion, gold and silver filled the vacuum. Jewellery was melted down into coins. Barter networks included small silver weights as a reference medium. In post-Soviet Russia, gold became a trusted unit during the rouble's volatility. In the United States during the Great Depression, private gold holdings were so widespread that the government resorted to forced confiscation under Executive Order 6102. That order alone is a powerful signal—not of gold's irrelevance, but of its threat to monetary monopoly.

Even in more subtle cases, gold plays a backstage role in state strategy. Central banks, for all their proclamations about innovation, continue to accumulate bullion. The People's Bank of China and the Russian Central Bank have expanded their gold reserves significantly in recent years—not as a bet on growth, but as a hedge against geopolitical risk and dollar weaponisation. That central banks, with their teams of economists and access to elite capital markets, still choose to store metal in vaults should arrest any notion that gold is merely symbolic. *It remains the fallback asset of those who understand the stakes of systemic rupture.*

Precious Metals vs Paper Promises

A defining trait of precious metals is that they are *nobody else's liability.* A bond, a bank deposit, or a pension is ultimately a promise—reliant on an issuer's solvency and political will. Gold and silver require no such promise. They do not default. They do not dilute. They do not go bankrupt. This singular quality gives them a unique profile in a fragility-aware portfolio.

In financial terms, metals are *uncorrelated.* They may not outperform equities in a bull market, but they shine in chaos. Their value is often counter-cyclical to trust-based systems. When confidence evaporates, metals ascend—not because they create value, but because they *hold it.* That holding function is what makes them indispensable in environments where digital systems are overexposed.

Consider the risks now embedded in modern finance: bail-ins, negative interest rates, capital controls, account seizures, and rising financial surveillance. In such an environment, the ability to hold value *outside the system* becomes not just desirable but essential. And yet, few assets meet that criteria. Cryptocurrencies offer partial solutions but come with their own vulnerabilities: energy dependence, network visibility, and regulatory whiplash. Gold and silver, by contrast, are *immediately useful, physically portable, and institutionally neutral.*

The Psychology of Metal

Precious metals also serve a psychological function that is often overlooked in quantitative models: they *anchor perception.* In times of volatility, panic, or narrative manipulation, they offer a material reassurance that numbers on a screen cannot. Holding a gold coin in hand is a different experience than reviewing a portfolio statement. It *feels real,* because it is. And that tangibility becomes critical when abstractions begin to wobble.

Moreover, the effort required to acquire, transport, and store metals imposes a discipline that fiat and digital assets often lack. It forces intentionality. It demands custody strategy. It creates a friction that, paradoxically, enhances resilience. *In an age of click-and-forget investment, the physicality of metals restores strategic awareness.*

Gold also acts as a psychological foil to hubris. It reminds us that trust-based systems are temporary, that no empire lasts forever, and that monetary systems are more fragile than they appear. For this reason alone, it deserves a place in any conversation about sovereign capital or antifragile wealth.

Critiques Worth Addressing

To engage the value of precious metals seriously, one must also address their limitations. Critics rightly point out that metals are illiquid in emergency scenarios, difficult to transport in large quantities, and vulnerable to confiscation. All of these concerns are valid—but *contextual.*

Liquidity, for example, is not binary. Gold may not be accepted at your local supermarket, but in black markets, global cities, or collapse scenarios, it is among the most tradable units of real value. Transport risk is real—but so is digital seizure. Diversification is the answer, not dismissal.

As for confiscation, history suggests that the threat is highest *after* metals have already proven their value. Governments confiscate gold when they are desperate—not because gold is useless, but because it is *too useful.* The very fact that you must plan for state interference is a signal of the asset's power. It is better to own an asset that may one day be targeted than to hold only those assets the state has no reason to fear.

Integration into Modern Resilience Strategies

Modern wealth strategy often revolves around liquidity, yield, and scalability. But these metrics assume institutional continuity. For those building *resilience*, not just returns, different metrics apply. Portability. Anonymity. Permanence. Decentralisation. On these dimensions, gold and silver score higher than nearly any other asset class.

For those concerned about storage, modern solutions abound: private vaults in politically neutral jurisdictions, multisignature vault access, and fractional ownership structures. The logistics of precious metals are not trivial, but nor are they prohibitive. As with any other domain of strategy, sophistication increases with intent.

Critically, gold and silver are not binary allocations. They function best as *a layer* in a multidimensional portfolio—hedging tail risk, insulating against policy shocks, and providing optionality when other systems falter. They are not a religion, nor a panacea. But they are an *ancient answer to a modern problem.*

Final Thought

In a world of rising monetary abstraction—where central banks create liquidity by fiat, currencies float without anchors, and institutions increasingly overpromise—the value of holding something real, finite, and enduring is not nostalgia. It is strategy.

Precious metals are not about longing for the past. They are about preparing for the *possible*. And in that sense, they remain not just relevant—but foundational.

When you can no longer trust systems to protect your wealth, you return to what *can't be corrupted by policy, politics, or promises*. You return to metal.

Building a Poly-Currency Mindset

Why thinking in only one currency is not just naïve—it's dangerous

At the heart of every collapsed economy is not simply a failed currency, but a failed imagination. Most people don't go bankrupt in financial crises because they had no assets. They go bankrupt because their *thinking* was denominated in a single system that no longer functioned. It is not the absence of money that ruins people; it is the belief that money means only one thing, in one form, from one issuer.

To think in just one currency—be it the dollar, the euro, the pound, or any fiat denomination—is to be intellectually disarmed in a world of shifting trust, political interference, and accelerating technological disruption. *A poly-currency mindset is not a hedge; it is a foundational upgrade in economic literacy.* It is the ability to perceive, navigate, and store value across multiple paradigms, recognising that monetary regimes are neither static nor sacrosanct.

This article aims to make that mindset concrete—not as an abstraction, but as a practical framework for those serious about resilient wealth.

Currency Is Not Money. Money Is Not Value.

Let us begin with clarity. A currency is not money. And money is not value. These distinctions are rarely made in everyday discourse, but they are critical if one is to think clearly about financial sovereignty.

A currency is a tool—a state-issued medium of exchange that is legally enforced. Money, more broadly, is any medium that fulfils three functions: a store of value, a unit of account, and a means of exchange. Value itself, however, is prior to both. It is social, subjective, and deeply contextual. *To equate value with a nation's fiat is to mistake the menu for the meal.*

When governments overprint, inflate, freeze, or devalue their currencies, the underlying value has not vanished—it has merely moved elsewhere. In such moments, those who survive are not necessarily those with more capital, but those with *more cognitive flexibility*. They know where value is *migrating to*, not where it used to be.

Case Studies: When Thinking in One Currency Destroyed Fortunes

Consider Argentina in 2001. The peso was pegged 1:1 to the US dollar. For nearly a decade, Argentine citizens were assured that their savings were safe. But when the peg collapsed and bank withdrawals were frozen (the infamous *corralito*), those who thought exclusively in pesos found their wealth cut in half—overnight. In contrast, those who had shifted savings into dollars, real estate, or even commodities retained purchasing power. The crisis wasn't merely financial. It was *epistemic*. The cost was paid by those who failed to mentally exit a system already on fire.

Or Zimbabwe in the 2000s. As hyperinflation devoured the Zimbabwean dollar, ordinary citizens turned to barter, gold, and foreign cash. Street vendors started quoting prices in US dollars, while government salaries remained in rapidly devaluing local notes.

A bifurcated economy emerged, and the ability to *translate mentally* across these domains became a survival skill.

These examples are not relics of exotic failures. They are rehearsals for a future in which monetary plurality becomes the norm, not the exception.

The Psychological Trap of Monetary Monoculture

Humans crave simplicity. One currency. One price. One account. But this psychological craving makes us intellectually lazy and dangerously exposed. Economists call it *unit-of-account bias*—the tendency to evaluate all prices and assets through a single frame, even when that frame is distorted or manipulated.

This bias is what makes inflation so effective. A person earning £100,000 per year may not feel poorer if their salary remains nominally the same—even if their rent, food, and transport rise 30% in real terms. They are measuring wealth by an *illusion*, not by function. A poly-currency thinker, by contrast, would immediately ask: *What else could this be priced in? What happens if I translate this into gold, Bitcoin, calories, or hours of labour?*

This mindset doesn't require one to abandon fiat. It requires one to see fiat for what it is: *one operating system among many*. And like all systems, it is optimised for the issuer, not the user.

Value Across Systems: Understanding Monetary Relativism

We do not live in a single economy. We live in overlapping economies with different rules, incentives, and degrees of coercion. The formal banking system. The shadow banking system. The crypto ecosystem. Black markets. Grey markets. Gift economies. Token economies. Reputation-based economies.

Each has its own "currency" of value. And these currencies—dollars, sats, gold ounces, hours, likes, favours—are not interchangeable. Their power comes from *context.* The ability to navigate this complexity is not a luxury skill. It is a sovereign one.

To think poly-currency is to ask:
– *What does value look like here?*
– *Who determines the rules of exchange?*
– *Is this system growing, stable, or collapsing?*
– *What are the conversion costs—financial, legal, psychological—between systems?*

Those who ask these questions do not merely protect their wealth. They *reposition themselves inside value itself.*

Building the Poly-Currency Toolkit

How does one cultivate this mindset practically?

It begins by *disentangling self-worth from state currency.* A salary in pounds is not your value. A savings account in dollars is not your security. These are temporary vessels. Start measuring assets and liabilities in multiple units: ounces of silver, kilowatt-hours, land, BTC, even reputation. Practice translating between them. Learn what each buys, where, and with whom.

Next, diversify not just assets, but *denominators.* Don't just buy Bitcoin; start thinking in satoshis. Don't just hold gold; learn to price goods in grams. Don't just trade crypto; understand the psychology of DeFi communities. The goal is not to worship any particular currency, but to build fluency across systems.

Then, *develop exit strategies* across domains. If one system fails—fiat, banking, blockchain—what's your access point to another? Can you move liquidity, even at frictional cost? Can you operate in informal economies if required? The poly-currency mindset is not about chasing returns. It's about ensuring *continuity under constraint.*

Tensions and Trade-offs

Poly-currency thinking also introduces a deeper, more philosophical awareness: *no system is value-neutral.* Every currency embeds assumptions about power, trust, and design. Fiat assumes state legitimacy. Bitcoin assumes decentralised consensus. Precious metals assume physical custody. Barter assumes social capital. None are perfect. All have risks.

The danger lies not in choosing wrong, but in choosing *only one* and becoming ideologically committed to its mythology. Those who believed the dollar would always rule the world failed to see the geopolitical decentralisation now underway. Those who thought Bitcoin was impervious to regulation have watched state-level chokepoints emerge in custody, taxation, and exchanges. *Every currency has a kill switch—it just resides in a different place.*

The Ethical Layer: Value Beyond Price

Finally, a mature poly-currency mindset extends beyond economics into ethics. When you stop thinking in one currency, you begin to see how much of modern value exchange is distorted by convenience or coercion. Is that "cheap" product priced in dollars, or in slave labour? Is that government stimulus true liquidity, or deferred taxation? Is your social capital growing in fiat terms while your moral capital is in deficit?

Wealth is not just what you can spend—it's what you can live with. And different currencies carry different ethical weights.

By consciously choosing your currencies—literal and metaphorical—you begin to reclaim value not just as a number, but as a worldview.

Final Thought

The world is not converging toward one system. It is diverging into many. Some digital. Some physical. Some legal. Some informal. *To think in only one currency today is to navigate the world with one eye shut and both hands tied.* It is not sophistication that enables poly-currency fluency—it is *humility*.

Value does not live in systems. It lives in people, places, skills, networks, and trust. Currencies are tools. And tools, when broken, must be replaced—not worshipped.

If the first stage of financial awakening is realising you're inside a game, the second is learning that there are many games. The poly-currency mindset is how you stay free—no matter which game breaks next.

Chapter 6
Hiding in Plain Sight

The central myth of modern finance is this: that what can be seen is what can be trusted. That legitimacy demands transparency. That wealth, to be considered real or respectable, must live in a balance sheet, pass through sanctioned hands, and glow dutifully under the institutional spotlight. It's a tidy belief—neatly packaged by tax authorities, regulatory frameworks, and the gleaming facades of high-street banks. But like many tidy beliefs, it doesn't survive contact with the world as it actually is. Or rather, the world as it's rapidly becoming.

In truth, visibility has become a risk.

We now inhabit a financial environment where to be seen is, increasingly, to be targeted. Digital footprints persist longer than paper trails ever did. Jurisdiction is no longer a boundary but a bureaucratic suggestion. From automatic account monitoring to international data-sharing pacts, from blacklisted blockchain addresses to the Kafkaesque reach of asset seizure laws—what once might have been dismissed as paranoia has become the new normal. The presumption is not of innocence, but of availability: every account discoverable, every transaction interrogable, every store of value potentially suspendable.

For those who still aspire to the status of a sovereign individual—and that notion is itself now contested—it is time to reframe. Not in the name of evasion, but of intention. The question isn't "How do I disappear?" It is, rather, "How do I design a life in which what truly matters cannot be taken from me at the flick of a switch?"

This chapter ventures into that reframe.

It offers no sanctuary for illegality, nor does it peddle the illusion of total anonymity. What it does propose is something subtler, and perhaps more powerful: the practice of lawful concealment. The kind of concealment that doesn't flout the law, but instead exploits the blind spots built into every system—those quiet seams where geography, legal nuance, and technology meet.

It is a discipline. A strategic art form.

It means constructing wealth that moves without fanfare. Assets that don't need applause. Structures that function in silence, not because they are hiding something shameful, but because not everything need be broadcast to earn its right to exist. It involves making use of tools—corporate entities, international custodians, encrypted protocols—not to dodge responsibility, but to place essential distance between self and system. A firewall, if you like, between the intimate and the interrogable.

And crucially, it means understanding that privacy and secrecy are not synonyms. To be private is to be deliberate. To be secretive is to be evasive. One is grounded in design, the other in fear. The aim here is not to vanish. It is to remain confidently visible, while ensuring the levers of your continuity are not easily grasped by others.

This is architecture, not escape. It is the quiet mastery of knowing what to disclose, and what to reserve—of making yourself legible only to the extent that it serves you. Beyond that, nothing.

The False Binary: Visibility or Illegitimacy

Let us begin by dispelling the false binary that dominates conventional thinking: that wealth is either visible and legitimate, or hidden and illicit. This framing, propagated by institutions and amplified by pop culture, has conditioned the public to equate privacy with guilt. It has normalised the idea that only criminals seek financial discretion.

But historically, discretion was a hallmark of wisdom, not deception. Aristocratic families, sovereign states, and successful merchants operated across layered jurisdictions and maintained complex structures not to defraud, but to *preserve.* Discretion was not secrecy—it was strategy.

In today's hyper-digitised world, we must reclaim that nuance. Hiding in plain sight does not mean obscuring assets from rightful scrutiny; it means ensuring that *no single point of failure—no institution, government, or algorithm—can unilaterally seize, suspend, or surveil the totality of your wealth.*

Three Dimensions of Concealment

This chapter unfolds in three tightly interconnected dimensions: digital, legal, and geographic.

1. Digital Camouflage

The first frontier is *code.* Increasingly, assets no longer live in vaults or under mattresses—they live in private keys, multisig wallets, decentralised exchanges, and distributed storage. But decentralisation, though powerful, is not privacy. Nor is encryption synonymous with safety.

We will explore how decentralised storage can be made resilient, how non-custodial financial tools offer true ownership without reliance on compromised intermediaries, and how digital camouflage is not about being invisible—but *indistinct.* When your asset looks like noise, it becomes harder to freeze, frame, or coerce.

The goal is not to vanish from the network. It is to move *within* it, unobserved, like data that cannot be categorised.

2. Legal Structures with Layers

The second layer is *structure.* Most people think of legal entities—trusts, foundations, companies—as administrative tools. In fact, they are jurisdictional technologies. They encode the priorities of their originating legal system and can be deployed, nested, and adapted to create legitimate buffers against predatory taxation, political instability, or arbitrary asset seizures.

But more structure is not always better. Complexity without clarity can be fatal. What matters is *strategic layering*—using multiple legal domains to ensure that *no single authority has holistic visibility or jurisdictional dominance over your wealth.* We will examine how savvy individuals use layered legal frameworks not to "hide" wealth, but to *de-risk it* from capture.

This is not about offshoring for show. It is about the intentional use of law as infrastructure.

3. Geographic Arbitrage of Safety

The third and most misunderstood domain is *geography.* Geographic arbitrage is often framed in simplistic terms—move to Dubai, invest in Singapore, store gold in Switzerland. But this misses the point.

Safety is not static. A country that is safe for corporations may be hostile to individual privacy. A jurisdiction favourable to gold may be inhospitable to crypto. A low-tax nation may become a high-risk one the moment capital controls are triggered.

Geographic arbitrage is not about choosing one safe haven. It is about distributing risk *across legal, political, and cultural environments*, in ways that do not correlate. We will explore how this approach—far from being exotic or paranoid—is now mainstream among international families, digital nomads, and even institutional investors.

The wise no longer think in terms of "my home country" and "abroad." They think in terms of *sovereign layers*—each with its own risk profile, and each acting as a shield for different parts of their asset base.

The Ethics of Discretion

One of the most important themes running through this chapter is ethical sophistication. This is not a book for those seeking to hide wealth to escape civic responsibility. It is for those who recognise that *systems themselves can become unethical*, and that blind compliance to unethical systems is not virtue—it is cowardice.

When legal regimes become tools of political retribution, when institutions weaponise compliance to extract leverage, and when financial systems are designed to penalise independence, *discretion becomes moral.* Not because it enables wrongdoing, but because it *preserves the space for doing right.*

The sovereign individual must always be more ethical than the system they operate in. And that often requires building buffers—of legal insulation, informational asymmetry, and cross-border optionality.

A Note on Simplicity and Resilience

There is a risk that readers interpret this chapter as a call for baroque complexity. That would be a mistake. The point is not to build an unbreakable labyrinth—it is to *design for resilience.* Simplicity, when built on sound structure, is more powerful than opacity. But *true simplicity is never simplistic.* It is engineered. Deliberate. Multi-layered.

We will return often to this idea: *Resilience is not redundancy. It is modularity.* A resilient wealth structure can bend without breaking, shift without collapsing, and remain invisible without disappearing.

What the Reader Will Gain

By the end of this chapter, the reader will:

– Understand how digital assets can be shielded without isolating them
– Gain clarity on legal entity design for asset protection and succession
– Learn how to use multiple jurisdictions to reduce visibility without losing control
– See examples from historical and modern contexts where discretion proved decisive

– Confront the ethical line between evasion and sovereignty—and know how to walk it with confidence

More importantly, readers will begin to *see visibility itself as a design decision*—not a default.

Final Thought

To "hide in plain sight" is not to disappear. It is to master *where you are visible, to whom, and under what terms.* It is to accept that power now lies with those who can *manage exposure*, not those who can maximise display.

This is the art of modern sovereignty. It begins here.

The Discreet Asset Doctrine

Protecting Wealth Through Strategic Invisibility, Not Secrecy

Wealth is not merely what you own—it is what you can *retain* under pressure. And in a world where visibility increasingly equals vulnerability, the most enduring wealth is not locked away in secret—it is *structured never to appear as a target in the first place.*

The common mistake among those new to asset protection is to conflate secrecy with safety. They imagine security as concealment, layering assets under shell companies, encrypted keys, or quiet jurisdictions. But true resilience does not lie in secrecy—it lies in *strategic invisibility.* Not hiding, but *not being noticed.* Not burying value underground, but ensuring that what's visible to others is *not what's vulnerable to them.*

This is the heart of the Discreet Asset Doctrine: the discipline of engineering wealth so it is *undetectable in its significance*, irrelevant to predators, and functionally inaccessible to arbitrary power. Its premise is neither ideological nor evasive—it is practical. And increasingly, it is essential.

Visibility Is a Modern Liability

The systems we interact with—financial, governmental, legal—are built to interpret visibility as compliance. But this assumption breaks down in crises. When regimes shift, when institutions collapse, or when policies turn predatory, *visibility becomes exposure.* The exposed become the taxed, the frozen, the seized, and the coerced.

Consider Cyprus in 2013, where bank account holders watched up to 47.5% of their deposits above €100,000 vanish overnight through a "bail-in". Or India in 2016, where 86% of the nation's cash was declared invalid with four hours' notice. In both cases, wealth that was visible—whether to a central registry or a central bank—was wealth that could be *violated.* No warning. No defence. No recourse.

The Discreet Asset Doctrine is a pre-emptive antidote to this condition. It teaches the affluent and the alert to build structures that *do not provoke notice* and *cannot be easily politicised, digitised, or centralised.* It is about owning nothing exploitable while controlling everything essential.

Secrecy vs Invisibility: A Distinction with Consequences

Secrecy implies intent to conceal something sensitive. It often involves misleading omissions or opaque legal mechanisms. And ironically, in an age of algorithmic scrutiny, secrecy triggers flags.

Strategic invisibility, by contrast, operates in the open—but reveals *nothing of consequence.* It leverages legal norms, jurisdictional diversity, and information asymmetry to make the asset irrelevant to external eyes. You *appear legible*, yet what matters most is *positioned out of reach.*

An asset is strategically invisible when:
– It is held through legal structures that separate beneficial ownership from operational control
– Its jurisdictional footprint limits exposure to any single tax, legal, or political regime
– Its digital or physical form is not easily monetised, frozen, or

traced
– Its existence is normal, but its significance is unknown

This isn't paranoia—it's prudence.

The Psychology of Targeting

When wealth is seized, it is rarely a purely economic act. It is *psychological.* Predatory states, failing institutions, and litigious adversaries go after what is *easy to find and emotionally satisfying to punish.* That means luxury properties, brokerage accounts, and business holdings with brand equity or visible profits.

What they overlook—or cannot access—is the capital structured as *non-liabilities*, held in low-drama jurisdictions, or functionally obfuscated through layered ownership. The best protection is often not to appear "protected" at all, but *uninteresting*—financially mundane, legally unenticing, jurisdictionally inconvenient.

This is why the Discreet Asset Doctrine requires behavioural restraint. It's not just about how assets are held. It's about *how the owner appears to live.* If your lifestyle demands constant validation—status vehicles, Instagram visibility, conspicuous generosity—you have already rendered yourself visible and exposed. The doctrine demands a quieter posture.

Historical Precedent: Discretion as Survival

History is not short on examples. In Nazi-occupied Europe, Jews who survived asset seizures were often those who had converted wealth into culturally invisible forms—jewellery repurposed as heirlooms, gold melted into tools, deeds transferred quietly to trusted allies. In Argentina's 2001 collapse, small business owners who had diversified into tangible but inconspicuous assets—land, tools, commodities—fared better than those with visible bank wealth. In modern Russia, oligarchs who relocated their assets into Western legal frameworks with layered trust structures often retained more wealth than those who relied solely on raw financial secrecy.

The lesson is consistent: *the wealth that survives is not necessarily the best-performing. It is the least visible to the forces of collapse.*

Legal Structures as Veils, Not Vaults

Legal entities are often misunderstood. People view trusts, foundations, LLCs or IBCs as vaults—hard containers where wealth sits. This is flawed. *They are veils*—meant to distort the visual field of adversaries, not merely to contain valuables.

A Cayman trust does not "hide" wealth—it *recontextualises ownership*. A Liechtenstein Stiftung does not protect capital through secrecy—it protects it through *non-equivalence*: you are not the legal owner, but retain strategic influence. Done properly, these structures render the wealth *legally irrelevant to attacks* even when visible.

This subtlety is what separates compliant structuring from reactive evasion. The Discreet Asset Doctrine insists that *the structure itself must be legitimate, public if necessary, but conceptually uninviting*. You build with law, not against it.

Modern Tools of Strategic Invisibility

A few contemporary tools illustrate this doctrine at work:

– **Cold storage multisig wallets**: decentralised control over crypto assets where no single person or server has access—rendering confiscation legally and technically non-trivial.

– **Dual citizenship with private banking rights**: enabling the allocation of wealth in jurisdictions disconnected from your country of residence, reducing unilateral risk exposure.

– **Layered operating companies**: creating visible commercial activity in one country while upstream ownership is routed through neutral, asset-protective jurisdictions.

– **Private credit funds**: investments that generate yield but are structured through limited partnerships or non-public vehicles, disincentivising legal targeting.

None of these instruments require hiding. They require *forethought.*

Strategic Invisibility in the Digital Age

Digital architecture is eroding traditional privacy. Every transaction, login, location ping, or device link creates an evidentiary trail. But digital opacity is still achievable—when *non-correlation* is prioritised.

For instance, purchasing crypto peer-to-peer, storing keys offline, and using decentralised protocols for transaction obfuscation—*not to hide*, but to *detach your actions from your identity.* When paired with jurisdictional diversification and lifestyle moderation, this digital discretion becomes immensely powerful.

Equally, investing in tokenised assets where ownership is fragmented across a DAO or non-custodial vehicle can protect you not through obscurity, but *through architectural indifference.* If your assets can't be meaningfully identified or extracted by any single party, they are less likely to be targeted.

Ethical Reflection: Visibility as a Design Choice

One of the most important shifts in mindset is this: *visibility is not a default. It is a design choice.* Most people do not realise how many of their financial behaviours are voluntary disclosures—KYC, open banking APIs, mortgage applications, property registries.

The Discreet Asset Doctrine teaches you to assume nothing is private unless engineered to be. And more importantly, it teaches that *not all privacy is secrecy.* Just because your assets are not legible to every institution does not mean they are hidden. They are simply *protected by layers of jurisdiction, logic, and discretion.*

This distinction is vital for legality and ethics alike.

Closing Insight

The goal is not to be untraceable. The goal is to be *uninteresting to trace.* The most protected wealth does not shout "protected"—it whispers *irrelevant.* Not because it lacks value, but because its form, structure, and placement render it *inert to arbitrary interference.*

To practice the Discreet Asset Doctrine is to accept that exposure is the new risk, and to engineer wealth that is *resilient by design, not just by intention.*

Because the future will not reward the visible. It will reward those who knew how to be present without being predictable—and valuable without being vulnerable.

Digital Camouflage

How Strategic Invisibility in the Digital Realm Protects Real-World Assets

There is a dangerous assumption embedded in modern asset protection: that digitisation and exposure are synonymous. That to hold wealth in digital form—whether currency, contracts, or credentials—is to accept vulnerability as the price of participation. But this assumption is outdated. The truth is sharper, more subversive, and ultimately more empowering: *what you digitise can disappear—not through secrecy, but through structure.*

This is the promise of *digital camouflage*—a sophisticated set of techniques, protocols, and philosophical shifts that allow individuals to participate in the digital economy without being exposed to its worst risks. It is not about hiding information. It is about *removing its central points of failure.*

In this chapter, we dissect how decentralised storage systems, non-custodial financial structures, and asymmetric information design can create *resilient, private, and border-agnostic* asset strategies. Not because they are invisible to everyone—but because they are *functionally irrelevant* to adversaries.

Why Custodians Fail

To understand the value of non-custodial frameworks, one must first appreciate the fragility of custodial systems. Banks, exchanges, cloud providers, and payment processors—all custodians—are, by design, *choke points.* They offer convenience, yes, but they also act as *gatekeepers of access.*

And gatekeepers are liabilities.

In 2022, the Canadian government invoked the Emergencies Act to freeze bank accounts of protestors and donors—*without court orders.* In 2023, Nigeria imposed withdrawal limits and phased in a centralised digital currency, narrowing access to one's own cash. Across jurisdictions, regulatory regimes are increasingly merging financial compliance with ideological conformity.

This is not paranoia. It is policy. And it underscores a critical truth: *If you need permission to access your own assets, you do not own them. You are renting access.* Digital camouflage begins where custodians end.

The Architecture of Non-Custodial Control

To operate in a non-custodial framework is to *disintermediate access to value.* You do not rely on a third party to hold or approve your transactions. You control the keys. You manage the risk. You design the redundancy.

Take Bitcoin—not as a speculative asset, but as a blueprint. A properly configured multisignature wallet, held across jurisdictions and hardware devices, creates a form of capital that is:

– Not dependent on any single server or government
– Not reversible or censorable by banks or regulators
– Not easily discovered unless deliberately disclosed

This is not "hidden" money. It is *uncorrelated money.* It exists on a public ledger, yet cannot be accessed or confiscated without keys that are often *geographically and mathematically fragmented.*

Apply this logic to data storage, and you get similar results. Platforms like IPFS (InterPlanetary File System) or Filecoin distribute encrypted fragments of files across hundreds of nodes. No single server contains the full document. No central operator can revoke access. The result is a *trust-minimised environment* where the user regains sovereignty over their information.

That is the essence of digital camouflage: *decentralisation not as ideology, but as survivability architecture.*

From Asset to Access: The Camouflage Mindset

Effective camouflage requires a mindset shift: from "what I own" to "what I control". It's not just about the form of the asset—but how it is accessed, transferred, and interpreted by third parties.

A gold bar in your name in a vault in London is exposed—because its custody and title are discoverable. But a tokenised claim to a pooled bullion asset, held through a DAO (Decentralised Autonomous Organisation) and linked to a smart contract requiring quorum approval for release? That's a different species. It doesn't merely obfuscate ownership. It *renders the idea of ownership more complex and less exploitable.*

This is not evasion. It's evolution. When designed well, digital camouflage doesn't hide the asset. It *dissolves the attack surface.*

Case Study: Tornado Cash and the Politics of Anonymity

In August 2022, the US Treasury sanctioned Tornado Cash, an Ethereum-based privacy protocol, for allegedly enabling money laundering. The move was unprecedented—not against a company, but *against code.* Smart contracts with no central authority were blacklisted. Developers were arrested. It was a watershed moment: privacy infrastructure was treated as criminal architecture.

But even in that environment, the principle held. Tornado Cash still operates at the protocol level. The contract lives on-chain. The keys are not held by a single actor. And despite the legal noise, users continue to route value through alternatives like zk-SNARK-enabled mixers or peer-to-peer protocols.

The lesson is critical: *Decentralisation can be criminalised, but it cannot be easily dismantled.* The more distributed the access logic, the harder it is to meaningfully suppress.

Digital camouflage does not rely on being allowed. It relies on being *resilient when permission is denied.*

The Three Layers of Camouflage

Digital camouflage functions best when layered across three axes:

1. **Infrastructure Layer**: Use decentralised protocols for storage, communication, and financial transactions. This means avoiding Google Drive, Dropbox, and centralised SaaS tools. Instead, leverage platforms like Skiff (for email), Arweave (for data permanence), and Monero (for private payments).

2. **Access Layer**: Obscure access routes. VPNs, Tor networks, burner hardware wallets, and air-gapped computers reduce digital fingerprints. Each step in your asset interaction chain should be uncorrelated from the last.

3. **Behavioural Layer**: Don't brag. Don't centralise. Don't repeat patterns. The best camouflage is lifestyle congruence. Appear modest, act boring, and structure ownership so that nothing about your digital behaviour suggests disproportionate control over valuable assets.

Visibility is not always the problem. Predictability is.

Ethical Considerations: Camouflage vs Obfuscation

It's important to distinguish *digital camouflage* from mere *obfuscation.* The former is architectural. It is about placing assets in contexts where their visibility carries no actionable consequence. The latter often implies active deception or criminal intent.

Camouflage is entirely compatible with legality. It can align with tax compliance, reporting standards, and regulatory frameworks—so long as those frameworks respect decentralised control. The goal is not to cheat the system. The goal is to *operate in systems where cheating is unnecessary because extraction is architecturally limited.*

This reframing is critical for professionals and entrepreneurs. You can hold crypto in cold storage. You can document beneficial ownership in a smart contract. You can conduct transactions through decentralised protocols. And you can do all of this *without violating a single law*—provided you design your systems to be *strategically robust, not simply secret.*

The Fragility of Centralisation in Crisis

Consider what happens when governments freeze capital outflows during a currency crisis. Think Argentina, Lebanon, or Zimbabwe. Citizens with local bank deposits are trapped. But those with decentralised assets—crypto wallets, tokenised commodities, encrypted data stores—retain optionality.

Not because they are invisible. Because they are *uncontrolled.*

Camouflage is not protection by distance. It is protection by *irrelevance to coercion.* It says: even if found, this cannot be used, frozen, or repurposed by you—because it is *not under your terms.*

And in a world where digital surveillance expands faster than digital ethics, that kind of architecture isn't a niche—it is a necessity.

Final Thought: Ownership Reimagined

The Discreet Asset Doctrine teaches us to separate possession from visibility. Digital camouflage extends this logic into the infrastructure of modern finance and information.

The question is no longer "Do I own this?" The better question is: *If someone tried to take this, what would they find? And would it matter if they did?*

In the next chapter, we explore how legal and jurisdictional layering can add depth to these strategies—turning digital camouflage into sovereign resilience. But first, remember: you do not need to hide from the world. You only need to *stop designing systems that depend on its permission to access your freedom.*

Legal Structures with Layers

How to Use Law as Armour, Not Just Paper

The single biggest misconception about asset protection is that it begins with secrecy. In truth, it begins with structure—and not just any structure, but one designed to *withstand scrutiny while deflecting coercion.* The most powerful forms of protection are not hidden—they are layered. Visible, compliant, and yet operationally elusive.

This is the quiet genius of *layered legal structures.* They are not loopholes or evasions. They are frameworks built precisely to endure under pressure: political, legal, or economic. And like all good architecture, their strength lies in how the parts relate—not just what they are.

This article is not a tutorial on shell companies or offshore banking clichés. It is an in-depth examination of how intelligent legal design creates *lawful insulation* around wealth—rendering it operationally inaccessible without violating due process, while keeping its owner well within the bounds of the law.

The goal is not to obscure ownership. It is to *transform ownership into control without exposure.*

The Fundamental Shift: From Title to Control

In modern legal systems, owning an asset—be it property, equity, or capital—means nothing if that ownership is *directly attributed* to you and *easily targeted* by creditors, regulators, or adversarial governments. Control is what matters. But the genius lies in separating the two: *you can control an asset without owning it in your name.*

This distinction is the foundation of layered legal protection. Trusts, foundations, holding companies, and multi-jurisdictional entities allow you to *relinquish legal ownership while retaining operational influence.* And that distinction is everything in a world where assets are increasingly subject to seizure not due to criminal conduct, but to political expedience.

Ask the former oligarchs of Russia. Ask the merchant families of Venezuela. Ask the business owners in Cyprus who saw "haircuts" imposed on bank balances during the 2013 financial crisis. *They didn't fail because they broke the law. They failed because their assets were too easy to reach.*

Trusts, Foundations, and the Myth of the "Offshore"

Let's begin with a critical clarification. Offshore is not illegal. Nor is it inherently unethical. In many cases, it is *legally prudent.* What matters is jurisdiction, purpose, and structure.

A trust, for example, is a legal relationship—not an entity. It allows one party (the trustee) to hold assets for the benefit of another (the beneficiary), often under conditions set out by a third (the settlor). Done properly, a trust:

– Removes the asset from your legal estate
– Protects it from personal lawsuits or political targeting
– Enables intergenerational continuity of control without probate or public visibility

A well-drafted discretionary trust with an independent trustee in a respected jurisdiction (e.g. Singapore, Liechtenstein, or New Zealand) creates a firewall: *you do not legally own the assets, but you benefit from them—contingently, not directly.*

Similarly, civil-law foundations—common in places like Panama or Liechtenstein—operate as *ownerless entities*. They are not controlled by shareholders. They act based on statutes set by the founder, which can include investment mandates, philanthropic goals, or succession plans. The founder doesn't own the foundation. Nor do the beneficiaries. It exists as its own legal organism.

This is not tax evasion. It is *estate architecture*—a way to protect capital from arbitrary forfeiture or political instability by reducing the *attack surface* of direct ownership.

Layering: Why One Structure Is Not Enough

A single trust or holding company, while helpful, is often insufficient. True protection arises when multiple legal entities are layered across jurisdictions, creating *juridical and procedural friction*.

Consider a simplified three-tier model:

1. A trust in New Zealand holds shares in…

2. A private interest foundation in Panama, which owns…

3. A holding company in the British Virgin Islands, which in turn controls…

4. Real estate or securities portfolios in your country of residence.

Each layer introduces a distinct legal jurisdiction, with its own rules on discovery, information exchange, and creditor access. A court in Country A cannot unilaterally compel disclosure from a foundation in Country B or enforce judgments against a trustee in Country C—unless coordinated through formal and often slow mutual legal assistance treaties (MLATs).

In short, *legal complexity becomes a time weapon*. It does not make assets untouchable. But it *delays*, *deflects*, and *discourages* opportunistic attacks—especially those driven more by political calculation than by genuine justice.

Law as a Defensive Weapon, Not a Loophole

The point is not to disappear from the system. It is to *weaponise compliance*. Everything in your structure should be:
– Legally declared where appropriate
– Taxed as required (but not more)
– Transparent to your advisors, but opaque to adversaries

This balance is the hallmark of modern strategic wealth planning. It says: "I will follow the rules of your game, but I will choose the board on which we play, and the ruleset under which outcomes are decided."

To do this, one must understand that legal structures are not static—they are *fluid mechanisms*. A trust can become irrevocable. A company can redomicile. A foundation can rotate its council. Each layer must be able to *evolve under pressure*, or it becomes brittle.

This is where most amateur planners fail. They optimise for the present, not for the worst-case future. They don't ask: *What happens if I am sued, politically targeted, or detained?* They don't plan for digital forensics, asset disclosure orders, or cross-border data-sharing agreements.

Layered legal design does.

The Role of Jurisdictional Arbitrage

Location matters—not just for taxes, but for *legal philosophy*. Anglo-common law, for instance, treats trusts with deep reverence. Civil-law systems often don't recognise them at all. Some jurisdictions value financial privacy; others default to automatic exchange of information under OECD mandates (e.g. CRS).

By selecting complementary jurisdictions—where asset-holding entities, trustees, and bankers are all subject to *non-overlapping disclosure rules*—one can build a structure that is *resilient to any single point of legal failure.*

This does not require exotic islands or secrecy havens. It can be done entirely within respected, white-listed jurisdictions. What matters is *how the parts interlock.*

Think like an engineer, not just a lawyer.

Ethical Reflection: Is This Just the Game of the Rich?

Critics often argue that such structures are only for the ultra-wealthy. That complexity is a form of privilege. That the ability to layer legal protections reflects an inequality of tools.

There's truth in that. But the deeper truth is more sobering: *the rules apply unevenly, whether you use them or not.* Complexity exists. Governments use it. Corporations use it. The question is not whether layered legal structures are fair—it's whether you want to operate in a system where *not using them means unnecessary exposure.*

In this sense, learning to layer your legal protection is an act of self-defence—not elitism.

It also compels ethical design. You can structure your wealth to *pay what you owe, protect what you've earned, and preserve what you want to pass on*—without feeding extractive regimes or becoming vulnerable to political blackmail.

Layering gives you options. Options are power. And power, when held by individuals with foresight and responsibility, can become *stability in an otherwise predatory world.*

Closing Thought: Transparency Is Not the Opposite of Protection

There is no contradiction between being transparent with tax authorities and being strategically invisible to attackers. The key is *who you disclose to, and under what terms.* With layered legal entities, you can file accurate disclosures, comply with regulation, and still design an architecture that limits exploitation.

That is the true genius of modern legal protection. Not hiding from the system—but *using the system to protect against its worst instincts.*

The next subchapter will explore how geographic location itself becomes a protective layer—how shifting your asset base, or even your personal base of operations, can create a jurisdictional firewall between you and those who would claim what you've built.

But for now, remember: *The paper trail is not your enemy. If structured properly, it is your shield.*

Geographic Arbitrage of Safety

When Sovereignty Is Strategy, and Geography Becomes a Firewall

We tend to think of geography as fixed: a passive backdrop to where we live, bank, or invest. In truth, geography is a form of *legal strategy.* Nations are not just places—they are legal codes, tax regimes, property rights traditions, and enforcement temperaments. And this matters profoundly, because *the same asset behaves differently depending on where it is located, regulated, or adjudicated.*

An ounce of gold in Argentina may be vulnerable to confiscation. The same ounce in Singapore may be legally and practically unreachable. A trust in California may be penetrable by a domestic court. A similar structure in the Isle of Man or Nevis may be functionally immune. A cryptocurrency wallet accessed from Iran can be frozen; the same wallet, accessed from a Swiss IP address with a Cayman-domiciled custodian, may be protected by layers of jurisdictional indifference.

This is the essence of **geographic arbitrage of safety**: *relocating assets, access, or structures in order to exploit the legal, political, or economic differences between nations.* It is not about running from regulation. It is about *choosing the regulatory framework most aligned with your values and vulnerabilities.*

The Premise: Jurisdictions Are Unequal by Design

There is no such thing as a truly global legal system. Every asset exists *somewhere*, and every somewhere comes with its own risks: judicial competence, political stability, creditor protection laws, capital controls, public registries, and susceptibility to geopolitical pressure.

What you "own" in one country can be nationalised, frozen, expropriated, or legally invalidated in another. And when crises hit—war, economic collapse, populist nationalism—the temptation of states to *redefine ownership* in their favour increases exponentially.

Modern history is littered with cautionary tales:

India, 1962: During the Sino-Indian War, the government froze all Chinese-owned bank accounts.

Zimbabwe, 2000s: Farmland owned by white Zimbabweans, often held under clear legal title, was seized en masse under land reform policies.

Greece, 2015: In the midst of a sovereign debt crisis, the government imposed capital controls, limiting cash withdrawals and overseas transfers.

Canada, 2022: The state froze bank accounts of citizens involved in politically controversial protests—not by court order, but through emergency administrative powers.

Each of these examples shares a core insight: *geography is not a neutral container.* It is an actor in your financial life. And when the state becomes adversarial—or simply unpredictable—your wealth is only as safe as the legal terrain on which it rests.

The Psychology of False Security

There is a comforting illusion in keeping one's assets "close to home". Familiar legal systems, local banks, property you can touch—it all feels more real, more controllable. But this intuition can be dangerously misleading.

Most people do not realise that domestic financial institutions are *extensions of state authority*. Banks are compelled to comply with court orders. Real estate registries can be edited by fiat. Securities can be frozen with a single legal notice. If all your assets are in one country—and particularly if you live in that country—you are *overexposed.*

Geographic diversification is not paranoia. It is *a hedge against concentration risk in legal systems.*

Imagine treating your sovereignty like a portfolio. Would you put 100% of your net worth in a single volatile stock, governed by a CEO with a history of arbitrary decisions, poor financial controls, and limited transparency? Of course not. Yet most people do precisely that with their national risk.

Jurisdictional Spread: Strategic Placement of Assets

The practical art of geographic arbitrage begins with understanding *what to place where.*

Bank Accounts: Holding a portion of your cash reserves in stable, low-debt jurisdictions—such as Switzerland, Singapore, or Liechtenstein—offers a buffer against domestic banking restrictions or currency collapse. These nations offer strong depositor protections and a track record of upholding private property.

Real Estate: Property in countries with strong rule of law (e.g., Portugal, New Zealand, or the UK) offers more than potential returns—it can serve as a residency pathway or second citizenship route. Conversely, property in emerging markets should be held via offshore entities to reduce exposure to local courts.

Corporate Entities: A holding company in a tax-neutral jurisdiction like the British Virgin Islands or Cayman Islands can centralise ownership of operating businesses in multiple countries, isolating legal risk and enabling flexible inter-company flows.

Digital Assets: Cryptocurrency custody is often dismissed as borderless. In reality, jurisdiction still matters. Hosting wallets with providers domiciled in jurisdictions that do not cooperate with your home country's asset recovery mechanisms can make the difference between resilience and forfeiture.

It is not about hiding—it is about configuring control across borders to dilute any one state's ability to unilaterally seize or disrupt your assets.

Case Study: A Venezuelan Entrepreneur's Escape Plan

Consider the case of a Venezuelan tech entrepreneur in 2015, whose company had grown substantially despite the country's spiralling economy. Fearing hyperinflation and capital controls, he took the following steps:

1. Registered a BVI holding company to own the IP and shares of the business.
2. Opened corporate bank accounts in Panama and Portugal.
3. Converted excess cashflow into Bitcoin, stored in a Swiss-custodied multi-signature wallet.
4. Acquired a small apartment in Lisbon to qualify for Portugal's Golden Visa, relocating his family preemptively.

When the Venezuelan bolívar collapsed and banks began restricting withdrawals, his peers were financially paralysed. He was not. *His safety was not geographic—it was architectural.*

The Ethical Imperative: Freedom Requires Optionality

This chapter is not about evading responsibility. On the contrary, *geographic arbitrage can be a moral tool.* In authoritarian regimes, activists, journalists, or businesspeople may find themselves targeted for reasons that have nothing to do with wrongdoing and everything to do with *disobedience.*

By internationalising assets, these individuals gain breathing room—*the power to walk away, to fund their cause, or to survive financially in exile.* The same logic applies to anyone seeking financial resilience: optionality is not a luxury. It is *a form of sovereignty.*

Moreover, the legal use of multiple jurisdictions creates competition between them. When capital can move freely, states are incentivised to treat their citizens better. Arbitrage is not only self-protective—it is *structurally reformative.*

Common Missteps and Practical Nuance

Not all internationalisation is wise. Poorly executed structures can:

Trigger tax complications

Violate foreign asset reporting laws

Create mismatched compliance obligations

The goal is not mere dispersion. It is *intentional placement based on legal resilience and access.* For example, keeping all offshore assets in a single country—say, Panama—may expose you to reputational or political shocks. Similarly, if all offshore banking is held in US dollars, you remain tethered to the US financial system—even if your bank is in the Caribbean.

Resilience demands not just location diversification, but *systemic diversification*: currencies, jurisdictions, legal regimes, and counterparty types.

Final Insight: The Geography of the Future Is Digital—but Still Territorial

While the digitisation of finance creates the illusion of placelessness, *jurisdiction still rules*. Even decentralised technologies are often anchored in physical realities: servers, development teams, legal incorporations, and custody layers.

Therefore, it is critical to map your financial architecture—not just by asset class, but by jurisdiction. Ask yourself:

Where is this asset legally domiciled?

What courts have authority over it?

What treaties bind its custodian?

Who can freeze, access, or repatriate it under pressure?

If you cannot answer those questions with precision, you are not safe. You are simply exposed in ignorance.

Geographic arbitrage is not escape. It is not avoidance. It is the *reallocation of exposure* in a world where sovereignty, law, and risk are no longer neatly confined to national borders.

What was once a privilege of the wealthy is now a survival skill for the informed. And in the decades to come, those who understand this logic will not merely endure disruption—they will *stand beyond its reach*.

Chapter 7
The Sovereign Portfolio

What if "wealth management" as we've known it no longer applied—not because wealth itself has vanished, but because the tools meant to steward it have fallen out of step with reality? The classic portfolio model presupposes a world that, frankly, no longer exists. It rests on assumptions that once made sense: credible institutions, uninterrupted access to capital, neutral jurisdictions, predictable governance. Those conditions might have held in the golden decades following the Second World War. But today? They are illusions, or at best, luxuries that can't be counted on.

The more pertinent question now isn't "What do you own?" It's: "What can you *reach*—and under whose terms?"

That's where the Sovereign Portfolio comes in. Not just as a shift in strategy, but as a wholesale rethinking of what wealth is *for*. The aim is not mere accumulation. It's architecture—designing capital in a way that is insulated from coercion, agile in the face of upheaval, and operable under your own agency. Wealth that doesn't simply exist on paper, but functions in the real world when the rules start to bend—or break.

At a glance, the sovereign portfolio may not look all that different from a conventional one. It could include the same categories of assets: equities, property, cash equivalents, digital stores of value. But the distinction isn't in the components. It's in the governing logic—*who controls what, and under what conditions.*

Traditional portfolios are built atop a scaffolding of third-party trust. Assets live within brokerages or custodial banks. Revenue flows through state-monitored channels. Withdrawals and transfers are subject to permissions—sometimes explicit, other times buried in the fine print. "Liquidity" is measured by market salability, not by actual, frictionless accessibility. You might have wealth. But you do not, in any meaningful sense, command it.

The sovereign approach flips this on its head. It asks a different set of questions: Can this be frozen? Can this be taxed arbitrarily? Can this be blocked, delayed, seized, or censored? If the answer is yes, then—by this framework—it's not truly yours. Control must be local, not abstract. Execution must be under your fingers, not at the mercy of a dashboard login and a terms-of-service agreement.

And this is not some libertarian flight of fancy. It's a practical response to an increasingly erratic landscape: capital controls, emergency powers, asset seizures, extraterritorial taxation, political deranking of accounts. A portfolio built for last century will not survive the dynamics of this one.

True sovereignty in wealth doesn't mean abandoning the system. It means standing adjacent to it, with options. It means holding assets in forms and locations that are hard to coerce and easy to move. It means cultivating income streams that can't be choked off at a single bottleneck. It means embracing legal, geographical, and technological pluralism—not as an ideology, but as insurance.

Because in the end, the foundational truth is disarmingly simple: if someone else can shut it down, then you're merely renting your security.

Wealth Without Gatekeepers: No Middlemen, No Permission

Let us begin where most portfolios fail—*custody*. In ordinary asset management, third-party intermediaries are the silent stewards of your capital. A brokerage account, a bank, a fund manager—each acts as a gatekeeper, holding title and access in your name, yet retaining decisive operational control.

In a normal environment, this works. In abnormal environments—and history teaches us they are never as far away as we think—it doesn't.

Consider the Canadian trucker protests in 2022. Regardless of one's view on the protest itself, what mattered from a financial sovereignty perspective was this: individuals had their personal bank accounts frozen for supporting a cause the government deemed destabilising. There were no trials, no financial crimes, just a state order—digitally executed, institutionally obeyed.

Or look at Cyprus in 2013, where bank depositors were subject to a "bail-in," and savings over €100,000 were confiscated to stabilise the banking sector. Or Nigeria's spontaneous currency redesign in 2023, which left millions unable to access cash as the state declared legacy banknotes void and delayed the distribution of new ones.

Self-custody is not about secrecy. It is about continuity. A sovereign portfolio eliminates reliance on permissioned institutions for access. This is why decentralised tools—cold storage wallets, encrypted credentials, direct title ownership, even bearer instruments—are not fringe ideas. They are *foundational infrastructure* for the modern portfolio builder who refuses to be a passive counterparty.

Income That Cannot Be Switched Off

The next fault line in the conventional model is income. Salaries, dividends, royalties—these are often dependent on structures that assume legal and political harmony. But *what happens when those structures falter?*

A sovereign portfolio includes *income streams that are not jurisdiction-bound, employer-dependent, or platform-constrained.* This does not mean abandoning the formal economy. It means *building a shadow layer of economic productivity that can survive disconnection.*

This can take many forms:

Location-independent consulting structured through offshore entities

Decentralised crypto staking or validator participation

Online IP royalties routed through global merchant accounts

Real asset rentals denominated in stable currencies outside your home nation

Algorithmic trading bots that require no human interface to generate yield

The shared characteristic here is *non-reliance on local continuity*. These streams do not hinge on any one jurisdiction's tax regime, employment laws, or bank solvency. They are *modular and migratory.*

The traditional model trains people to seek employment within a framework. The sovereign portfolio reorients the builder to *generate economic value that is not confined by any framework at all.*

This is not simply a hedge. It is a *form of freedom creation*—income that exists beyond borders, and beyond bureaucracy.

Liquidity Reimagined: The Triangular Framework

Liquidity is often misunderstood. Most investors define it as "the ability to sell." But true liquidity in sovereign architecture involves *the ability to convert, move, and control—rapidly, without notice, across systems.*

This requires what we might call the *Liquidity Triangle*—a structural distribution of wealth across three axes:

1. **Immediacy** – Assets you can access and convert within 24–48 hours, even under pressure (e.g., stablecoins in cold storage, foreign cash reserves, gold stored locally)

2. **Mobility** – Assets that can be transferred cross-border without institutional bottlenecks (e.g., private equity shares via smart contracts, decentralised digital assets)

3. **Anchors** – Durable stores of value that may not be rapidly liquid, but which preserve wealth across generational timescales (e.g., foreign real estate, physical precious metals, land, or enterprise equity)

Conventional portfolios often collapse this distinction. They might have liquidity on paper—such as public equities—but that liquidity is system-contingent. In moments of capital controls, market halts, or payment processor freeze, *paper liquidity becomes illusory*. Sovereign portfolios separate liquidity *by function*, not just by form.

This triangle also helps combat *reactionary behaviour in crises*. When panic strikes, people rush to liquidate indiscriminately. But if liquidity has already been *tiered strategically*, one can act with calm and clarity. Certain assets are for flight, others for continuity, others for legacy. *Each has its place in the choreography of chaos.*

Building Is a Mindset, Not Just a Method

To construct a sovereign portfolio is to rewire one's approach to wealth entirely. It demands unlearning what traditional finance teaches: that trust in systems equals security, that compliance equals stability, that diversification within one legal jurisdiction is enough.

It is not. Not anymore.

The sovereign portfolio is a *living system*, not a static allocation. It must be *tested regularly*—can you move it quickly? Can you verify it privately? Can you explain it to no one but still prove its integrity? Can it survive the revocation of permissions you take for granted—bank access, platform APIs, residency visas?

This is not abstract theory. This is the future of wealth protection—and for those paying attention, *it is the present of wealth engineering.*

Sovereignty, after all, is not granted. It is built.

This chapter unpacks how. You will learn:

Why third-party custody is a silent liability

How to structure borderless income that persists even when institutions fail

The principles behind tiered liquidity, and how to implement it in real-world terms

The psychological shift from asset accumulation to asset autonomy

Whether you are an investor, entrepreneur, or professional, these ideas are not optional reading. They are *core competencies for surviving financial modernity*—and more than that, they are *tools for thriving in post-institutional terrain.*

Let us begin.

Building a Freedom Stack

Engineering Resilient Wealth in a Fracturing World

Wealth is no longer about having more—it's about *needing less permission to use what you already have.* In a world defined not by abundance but by volatility, ownership alone is not enough. What matters is structure: *how your assets are layered, how accessible they are across borders, how visible they are to others, and how dependent they are on institutional trust.* This is the organising principle behind the Freedom Stack—a portfolio architecture built not around maximum returns, but around *maximal optionality.*

If the sovereign portfolio defines the mindset of the self-custodied individual, the Freedom Stack defines the *practical implementation.* It is not a single product, platform, or investment. It is a layered system—a carefully balanced, anti-fragile arrangement of assets designed to operate under radically different conditions. Economic normalcy. Political repression. Internet blackouts. Currency collapse. The Freedom Stack isn't built for one of these—it's built for *all of them.*

And like all robust systems, its power lies in redundancy and distribution. No single point of failure. No single centre of trust. No single location, currency, asset class, or governing regime.

To construct a Freedom Stack is to answer the question: *If everything failed tomorrow—banks, borders, brokers, bandwidth—what wealth would I still control?*

Rethinking Wealth from First Principles

The traditional portfolio is optimised for risk-adjusted returns in a stable system. It assumes functioning markets, enforceable property rights, and uninterrupted liquidity. The Freedom Stack discards these assumptions. It begins from a more sober baseline: *you are living in a world where continuity can no longer be taken for granted.*

This is not theoretical alarmism. It's empirical realism. Argentina froze bank withdrawals in 2001. Lebanese citizens lost access to savings during the 2019 financial implosion. Russian expatriates in 2022 found their brokerage accounts suspended—not by Russia, but by Western firms. American citizens abroad are often denied banking services altogether due to FATCA compliance risks. The modern investor lives at the mercy of overlapping jurisdictions, unpredictable sanctions, and opaque compliance regimes.

Thus, the Freedom Stack isn't about outsmarting the market—it's about *outlasting the system.*

The Architecture of the Stack: Function Before Form

To design a Freedom Stack, you don't begin with asset classes. You begin with *functions*. Ask: What does your portfolio need to *do*, under duress?

There are three foundational functions every sovereign-minded investor must fulfil:

1. **Preserve purchasing power across time**
2. **Ensure convertibility across borders**
3. **Maintain access without institutional approval**

From these three functions, the architecture of the stack emerges—layer by layer. Each layer must support a specific kind of resilience.

The Base Layer: Self-custodied hard assets
This includes gold, silver, and—in jurisdictions where feasible—privately held real estate. These assets are apolitical, uninflatable, and do not require third-party permissions to verify or access. They are not yield-bearing, but that is precisely their strength. *Their job is to exist through the storm.*

The Mobility Layer: Digital bearers of value
Cryptographic assets—Bitcoin, Monero, stablecoins on decentralised chains—reside here. These are transportable, concealable, and instantly convertible. Crucially, when stored non-custodially, they obey no banking holiday, sanction list, or geographical constraint. *This is your go-bag capital.*

The Income Layer: Autonomous revenue sources
These are systems that generate income independently of formal employment or local economies—distributed digital products, remote consulting, algorithmic trading bots, permissionless lending protocols. This layer ensures that you are not only storing wealth, but also producing it—*without needing approval, payroll systems, or corporate hierarchies.*

The Shelter Layer: Legal and geographic arbitrage
Trusts, foundations, multi-jurisdictional accounts, residency options, citizenship-by-investment programs. These don't generate income, but they *insulate it.* They place distance—legal, political, geographic—between you and potential threats. Their role is not yield but *defence.*

Each layer serves a distinct function. Each is governed by a different logic of access, control, and risk. The genius of the Freedom Stack is not in any single layer—it is in *how they interlock.*

Redundancy Is Not Inefficiency

To a conventional investor, the Freedom Stack looks inefficient. Why hold assets that don't yield? Why store capital in jurisdictions you don't live in? Why operate income streams in decentralised platforms when they're harder to scale?

But resilience is not efficient. It is *intentional slack*. Redundancy is not waste—it's insurance against failure.

Consider the submarine. It has multiple oxygen systems. Not because all are used daily, but because failure is catastrophic. The same applies to wealth architecture in the digital-financial age. If your assets exist on a single platform, under a single name, in a single country, under a single rule set—you are not diversified. You are concentrated in complexity.

The Freedom Stack builds for *resilience, not elegance.*

Visibility Is a Vector of Risk

Secrecy is not the goal. But *strategic invisibility* is essential. In the digital age, most assets are not stolen—they are *frozen, blocked, taxed into submission, or legally redefined.* Visibility, therefore, is a liability. The Freedom Stack deliberately varies its visibility across layers.

Your income-producing business may be public and compliant. Your hard assets should not be. Your digital mobility layer should be *uncorrelated to your legal identity.* Your legal structures should be *transparent but obfuscated in ownership.* This is not about hiding—it's about *minimising vectors of interference.*

You are not playing hide-and-seek with the state. You are building an architecture that *does not invite interruption.*

Ethical Wealth in a Systemically Hostile World

Some will argue that building such structures is unethical—that it's a form of evasion or systemic non-participation. But this critique presumes the system remains aligned with the individual. Increasingly, it is not.

When economic policy prioritises currency debasement, when legal frameworks enable asset seizure without trial, when financial institutions can block access without explanation—*exit becomes not avoidance, but moral necessity.*

A Freedom Stack is not a tool of the ultra-wealthy or the paranoid. It is a *practical strategy for individuals who recognise that financial safety is no longer a given.* And unlike the offshore games of past generations, this stack is *available to the digitally literate, globally minded, and jurisdictionally agile middle class.*

This is not about "escaping the matrix." It's about *outsmarting its constraints* with dignity and clarity.

Composability as a Skillset

You do not buy a Freedom Stack—you *build it.* Slowly, deliberately, over years. You learn how to custody your own keys. How to manage multiple tax residencies. How to structure contracts across jurisdictions. How to build income streams that do not rely on fixed locations. The process *builds you*, not just your net worth.

And the mindset shift is irreversible. Once you see wealth as *systems engineering rather than accumulation*, you cannot return to passive investing. You begin to ask different questions. Not "What return will this generate?" but "What threat does this neutralise?" Not "Is this yielding income now?" but "Can I access it when I need it most?"

You move from investing for growth to *engineering for resilience.* From hoping for safety to *designing for sovereignty.*

The Freedom Stack is not a hedge. It is not a portfolio tilt. It is a redefinition of wealth as *control under pressure.*

In the chapters ahead, we will examine how each layer functions in the wild. How decentralised tools can survive coordinated crackdowns. How legal structures can protect value even under reputational assault. How to construct personal liquidity systems that operate without reliance on any single financial pipeline.

But before that, ask yourself:

If everything you owned today became inaccessible tomorrow, what would still be yours?

If the answer is unclear, it's time to begin stacking.

No Middlemen, No Permission

The Case for Self-Custody and Decentralised Access

Modern finance operates on a quiet assumption: that you do not own your money. You *access* it, *request* it, *manage* it—through platforms, intermediaries, and institutions that hold the final word on when, how, and whether you may use what you believe is yours. A brokerage may halt withdrawals. A payment processor may freeze your account. A central bank may debase your purchasing power overnight. In this context, the concept of "ownership" is often an illusion—a confidence game contingent on uninterrupted institutional goodwill.

Self-custody challenges this paradigm at its root. It reasserts the ancient but radical principle that *true ownership requires no permission.* That the only secure wealth is that which you can access *unmediated,* without reliance on fragile trust networks or institutional benevolence. And with the rise of cryptographic tools and decentralised infrastructure, this principle is no longer philosophical. It is practical, scalable, and necessary.

The implications are profound—not merely financial, but psychological and political. Because when you remove the middleman, you do not just remove a transaction fee. You *remove a point of control.*

The Middleman is the Choke Point

Historically, intermediaries were necessary to enable commerce: clearing houses, escrow agents, banks, notaries. They provided trust where technology could not. But with the digitisation of finance came a subtle inversion: the middleman no longer just *facilitates* trust; he *commands* access.

Consider PayPal. In 2022, it briefly published a policy stating it could fine users $2,500 for "misinformation," withdrawn only after public backlash. Or look to Canada's 2022 trucker protests, during which the government directed financial institutions to freeze the bank accounts of protest supporters—without court orders. These are not isolated anecdotes. They are signals. *Access to your money can now be governed by your speech, your politics, your geographic location—even your social affiliations.*

The same applies to brokerages. During the 2021 GameStop short squeeze, Robinhood restricted trading on specific stocks under regulatory pressure, protecting institutional interests at the expense of retail traders. And across Europe and Asia, we've seen crypto exchanges forcibly close accounts tied to certain nationalities following sanctions or jurisdictional conflicts.

Your asset may be listed under your name, but its usability is licensed. And like any licence, it can be revoked.

Self-Custody: Control, Not Convenience

At the heart of the self-custody movement lies a deceptively simple idea: *If you don't hold the keys, you don't own the asset.* Whether it's Bitcoin, Ethereum, a stablecoin, or tokenised collateral, if it resides on a centralised exchange or hosted wallet, its existence is effectively *custodial.* It depends on servers you do not control, policies you cannot alter, and executives you do not elect.

This is not about ideology—it's about *operational control.*

Self-custody tools allow individuals to take cryptographic possession of their digital wealth. This is not equivalent to memorising a password. It is ownership enforced by *mathematics rather than by institutions.*

The simplest example: a hardware wallet. It stores private keys locally and offline. Even if the internet collapses or your service provider ceases to exist, as long as you possess your recovery phrase, your assets remain under your control.

But the principle extends further—into decentralised storage of documents, encrypted identity credentials, peer-to-peer communication tools, and even self-executing legal agreements. In each case, *self-custody transforms the individual from account holder to protocol participant.*

This shift carries a learning curve. It demands greater responsibility and offers fewer safety nets. But it also grants sovereignty in the deepest sense: *The ability to operate without seeking permission.*

Permissionless Systems: Access that Cannot Be Denied

Imagine attempting to send a bank transfer from Argentina to Nigeria during a currency crisis. Or withdrawing funds from a brokerage account while stranded abroad due to geopolitical conflict. Or accessing PayPal after having your account restricted due to algorithmic misflagging.

In such moments, the problem is not that your wealth has disappeared—it's that *you can't reach it.*

Permissionless systems such as Bitcoin or Ethereum solve this by eliminating the gatekeepers. They operate on decentralised consensus, not corporate policy. Once broadcast to the network, your transaction cannot be censored, delayed, or reversed. No central authority adjudicates your intent.

This doesn't guarantee success—it simply guarantees *equal footing.* And that's the key: *The system does not know who you are, only that your cryptographic signature is valid.*

To critics, this sounds risky—dangerous even. Surely anonymity enables crime. But this argument fails to ask the more foundational question: *What kind of system is acceptable for free people?* A system where privacy is preserved unless judicially suspended—or one where privacy must be requested and often denied?

Permissionless systems represent the financial analogue of freedom of speech. Not all speech is noble—but the capacity to speak without pre-clearance is what separates liberty from licence. The same is true for capital.

Self-Custody Is Not Isolation

A common mischaracterisation of self-custody is that it leads to financial isolation—hermetic users locked out of the broader system. In reality, the opposite is true.

By holding assets directly, users *gain flexibility* in choosing how and when to interface with institutions. A self-custodied crypto holder can still interact with exchanges, pay for services, even file taxes. The difference is that *they choose when, how, and under what terms.*

This asymmetry of control is no small matter. In traditional systems, your identity *is your access.* Lose your login credentials, and the institution may help you. But if the institution itself is compromised—or malicious—you have no recourse. With self-custody, *access is decoupled from institutional memory.* You are not at the mercy of help desks, compliance teams, or arbitrary policy shifts.

Moreover, the self-custodied individual can *interoperate across systems.* You can move assets from cold storage to decentralised finance protocols for yield. You can convert stablecoins into local currency when needed. You can engage with emerging tools like decentralised identity verification, web3 voting, and DAO governance—none of which require the permission of a gatekeeper.

The Psychological Shift: From Customer to Custodian

This transformation is not purely technical—it is *psychological.* Self-custody demands a shift in how individuals perceive their role. You are not a passive consumer of financial services. You are an active custodian of your own capital stack.

This entails risk—but also immense empowerment. With risk comes *literacy*, and with literacy comes *sovereignty.* You no longer outsource trust—you *design* it. You no longer delegate security—you *build* it.

And this shift is sticky. Once you learn to operate without middlemen, you begin to question other dependencies. Why must legal ownership be routed through a registrar? Why must identity be verified by a central database? Why must credit scoring be monopolised by opaque agencies? Each new capability reveals an older fragility.

Self-custody is not just about holding crypto. It is about holding *your autonomy.*

Challenges and Realities: Not All Access is Equal

To pretend that self-custody is universally viable would be dishonest. Key management is hard. UX is still evolving. Loss of seed phrases is a real and irreversible event. There are real barriers to entry: technical, educational, psychological.

Moreover, decentralised systems are not always decentralised in practice. Many "DeFi" applications depend on centralised front-ends. Many wallets rely on infrastructure hosted by third parties. And most users, understandably, prioritise convenience over sovereignty—until they're given a reason not to.

That said, *progress is rapid.* Social recovery mechanisms, multi-signature vaults, biometric seed phrase backups, decentralised inheritance systems—these tools are coming into focus. The direction of travel is unmistakable.

And the growing volatility of the institutional world—bank failures, inflation, regulatory overreach—is accelerating the need.

Final Insight: Sovereignty Begins at the Endpoint

Ultimately, the real revolution is not blockchain. Not tokens. Not finance. It is *architecture.* We are entering an age where the structure of systems matters more than the branding of services. And in this world, *middlemen are not just inefficient—they are existential liabilities.*

To build a sovereign portfolio, to construct resilient wealth, you must start at the root: *what you can access, without asking.* This is the irreducible baseline. Everything else is strategy layered on top.

No middlemen. No permission. Just access, control, and clarity.

You do not need to be rich to begin. You need to be ready.

Income Streams That Can't Be Switched Off

Frameworks for Developing Autonomous, Borderless Income

The illusion of security in modern income is often more comforting than it is accurate. Whether derived from employment, dividends, royalties, or government entitlements, most income today flows through centralised choke points—nodes of control that can restrict, suspend, or terminate access at will. A salary can be frozen. A platform can demonetise. A jurisdiction can impose capital controls overnight. Increasingly, individuals are discovering that the durability of their income is not defined by the amount earned, but by the *conditions under which it continues to flow.*

This chapter is not about getting rich. It is about staying solvent when systems falter, institutions retreat, or borders harden. It explores income not as a revenue stream to be maximised, but as a *resilience layer to be fortified.* Specifically, it introduces a portfolio approach to building income that is autonomous—independent of single points of failure—and borderless—immune to the arbitrary constraints of geography, ideology, or bureaucracy.

Autonomous income streams cannot be switched off because they are *not governed by permission.* They are antifragile not in their yield alone, but in their *architecture.* They are designed not for optimality under ideal conditions, but for continuity under pressure. This is the frontier of sovereign finance.

Centralisation Is the Weakest Link

To understand why autonomy matters, consider the typical income stack of a modern professional. Salary via employer. Savings in a bank. Investment returns via a brokerage. Perhaps some digital revenue via platforms like YouTube, Amazon KDP, or Substack. These streams feel diverse but are structurally centralised. Each relies on trusted third parties, intermediated infrastructure, and compliant identity layers. What happens when any node deactivates access? The income stops—often without recourse, regardless of the legality or merit of the suspension.

We've seen freelancers lose access to platforms due to algorithmic mislabelling. Content creators demonetised without due process. Academics banned from payment processors for political affiliations. Even pensions in some states are being subject to ideological screening. *The more global and digital the economy becomes, the more fragile the links in the chain become—unless they are deliberately decentralised.*

The challenge is not merely economic—it is existential. Income is what allows us to *navigate*, not just survive. When access to earning potential is arbitrarily interrupted, personal agency collapses with it. Which is why resilient wealth begins with *resilient income.*

Characteristics of Autonomous, Borderless Income

Not all income is created equal. What distinguishes switchable from unswitchable income is not quantity but *structure*. A robust income model has three defining features:

1. **Non-Custodial Access** – Income is received or accessible without intermediaries who can censor or delay it.

2. **Geographic Neutrality** – Income continues regardless of the earner's location or nationality.

3. **Permissionless Conversion** – The ability to transform earned value into usable currency without reliance on centralised clearing houses.

Let's break these down.

Non-custodial income means you control the keys. This is most evident in decentralised finance (DeFi), where protocol-based yield strategies can provide interest or staking rewards directly to a self-custodied wallet. It can also apply to crypto-native freelancing, where clients pay directly in stablecoins or BTC to a wallet without platform mediation.

Geographic neutrality is about jurisdictional redundancy. An affiliate marketer earning in US dollars through a Singapore-based payment gateway into a crypto wallet has more resilience than a civil servant paid only in local currency into a single domestic account. Likewise, a digital product business with global customers and multi-currency settlement options is structurally safer than one tethered to a local payment processor.

Permissionless conversion refers to the ability to swap one form of value for another without regulatory bottlenecks. Peer-to-peer (P2P) exchanges, decentralised trading protocols, and local crypto OTC (over-the-counter) networks all offer pathways to move capital without going through traditional banking rails. This is essential in situations where governments restrict FX (foreign exchange) transfers or impose capital controls.

These traits may sound technical or fringe—but they are rapidly becoming mainstream out of necessity. As the financial system fragments geopolitically, *designing income streams that are sovereign by default becomes a form of strategic survival.*

Frameworks for Income Sovereignty

Let's now look at concrete frameworks for building income that aligns with these principles. What follows is not a one-size-fits-all blueprint but a flexible set of lenses for evaluating and assembling resilient income.

1. The Modular Income Stack

Think of income as a stack—each layer supporting the others. A modular stack balances short-term cashflow with long-term capital growth, passive elements with active effort, and geographic diversification with jurisdictional safety.

Base Layer: Crypto-native earning or stable cashflow sources (e.g. remote freelance work, consulting, digital products, SaaS microservices).

Mid Layer: Staking, yield farming, or DeFi lending using self-custodied crypto assets to generate moderate return.

Top Layer: Asset-based income such as tokenised real estate, IP royalties, decentralised protocol rewards, or NFT licensing streams.

Each layer should be *detachable*—able to continue operating independently if one part fails. For example, if local banks freeze accounts, stablecoins should continue flowing via direct-to-wallet payments. If a jurisdiction imposes sanctions, other layers should be able to route income through alternative networks.

2. Jurisdictional Routing

Income sovereignty is often less about what you earn and more about *where it lands*. A freelancer paid in fiat to a US-based PayPal account is more vulnerable than one who invoices in USDC to a non-custodial wallet. An entrepreneur receiving affiliate revenue in Bitcoin via Strike or BTCPayServer is less dependent on banking APIs or card networks. In high-risk environments, *routing income through jurisdictions with digital asset clarity and privacy protections can be the difference between fluidity and forfeiture.*

Practically, this means maintaining multi-jurisdictional payment pathways, including:

Multiple crypto wallets across different chains

Bank accounts in stable jurisdictions

Off-ramp options in different regulatory zones

Dual payment processors (e.g. Stripe + crypto gateways)

Resilient earners do not just *accept* income—they *engineer* its flow.

3. Stateless Monetisation

The future of unswitchable income is stateless monetisation—the capacity to earn value without reference to national identity. This is not a political position. It is a design goal.

Platforms like Gitcoin, Ujo, Audius, or Mirror are early experiments in stateless monetisation. So is earning through DAO governance participation, liquidity provision incentives, or NFT minting royalties. These models use *wallets, not passports*, to define participation.

This is critical for individuals in countries with broken banking systems, hyperinflation, or repressive controls. Stateless monetisation allows them to access global demand directly and *be paid in forms of money that don't decay under local policies.*

Importantly, stateless income is not limited to crypto-native domains. It can include:

Remote work for foreign employers who pay in stablecoins

Consulting via blockchain-secured smart contracts

Licensing of digital assets (e.g. code, design, writing) via decentralised platforms

Offering services via privacy-respecting tools like Nostr or Signal for payment in BTC or Monero

It is the structural independence—not the novelty—that gives these streams their resilience.

Risks and Realities

None of this is utopian. Autonomous income does not eliminate risk; it *redistributes* it. Where traditional systems offer frictionless UX at the cost of surveillance and censorship, decentralised systems demand literacy, discipline, and vigilance.

Key management is unforgiving. Fraud is rampant in some crypto markets. Market volatility can undermine short-term stability. Regulatory hostility is unevenly distributed. And not all decentralised tools are truly decentralised in practice.

Moreover, building sovereign income requires time. It often begins as a side-project, not a full replacement. It grows in layers, through experimentation and failure. But its value compounds—not just economically, but psychologically. Each new channel reinforces autonomy.

The goal is not perfection, but *optionality*. Sovereign income is about *building routes out of dependence*, not severing ties with the existing system overnight.

Final Insight: Income is the First Layer of Exit

A sovereign portfolio is only as sovereign as its inflows. You cannot store, move, or protect wealth without a way to *earn it first.* Which is why income sits at the foundation of strategic independence.

In a collapsing or censorial environment, capital is not the first to be confiscated—*cashflow is.* If they can turn it off, they can control you. If they can't, they have to negotiate.

So the test is simple: *Can you still earn if your country shuts down banking rails? If your identity is flagged in a database? If your accounts are frozen?*

If not, you don't own your income—you lease it.

To build freedom, start with earnings. Not just higher—but harder to silence.

The Liquidity Triangle – How to Structure Assets for Rapid Movement and Long-Term Value

There is a subtle but defining distinction between wealth and usable wealth. Many asset holders mistake value on paper for financial power—until they attempt to move that value under pressure. It is here, in the constraints of liquidity, that wealth is either revealed as *resilient* or rendered inert.

Consider a successful entrepreneur with a £5 million valuation tied up in private equity, real estate, and locked pensions. On paper, they are affluent. But if forced to relocate within 48 hours—whether due to state seizure, political unrest, or a legal dispute—what fraction of that wealth can be accessed, mobilised, and protected? For most, the answer is disquieting.

The liquidity triangle is a strategic framework for resolving this tension. It teaches that *true capital power is not defined by what you own, but by how quickly you can reposition it across time, geography, and legal systems.* This framework challenges the static conception of asset allocation and replaces it with a dynamic design: one where liquidity, portability, and durability must be balanced deliberately.

This article is not about portfolio optimisation in the traditional sense. It is about financial *agility under pressure*. It introduces a three-part framework for structuring assets so they can flow under duress and compound value under stability. We will explore the characteristics of liquid capital, the trade-offs between speed and resilience, and the psychological illusions that undermine most asset holders. If there is one enduring idea, it is this: *static wealth is vulnerable wealth.*

Why Liquidity Matters More Than Ever

In ordinary times, the illiquidity of an asset is merely inconvenient. Selling a property may take months; unwinding a private equity position may require years. But in crises—whether personal, economic, or geopolitical—illiquidity becomes existential. You cannot evacuate across a border with fractional shares of an investment fund. You cannot negotiate with customs officers using a pension drawdown. In such moments, *capital that can't move is capital that no longer matters.*

History is full of examples where families, businesses, and entire classes were impoverished not because their assets disappeared—but because they became inaccessible. Wealthy German Jews in the 1930s were unable to liquidate their property before escape. In Venezuela and Lebanon, inflation trapped citizens in worthless bank balances, even while they technically held assets. In Cyprus, depositor bail-ins froze funds overnight. Across the Global South, land-rich families often live cash-poor due to structural illiquidity.

To assume that your assets will always be accessible on your terms is not just naïve—it is historically illiterate. Liquidity is what turns static capital into strategic agency.

The Three Sides of the Liquidity Triangle

The Liquidity Triangle consists of three dimensions: *Immediacy*, *Durability*, and *Portability*. Each asset class is evaluated on how well it performs across these vectors. The triangle is not just a classification tool—it is a design philosophy for sovereign asset architecture.

1. **Immediacy** – How quickly can the asset be converted into usable purchasing power?

2. **Durability** – How well does the asset preserve value over time and across crises?

3. **Portability** – How easily can the asset be transferred or reconstituted across borders and jurisdictions?

No asset scores perfectly across all three. The art of sovereign wealth design is in *balancing trade-offs to ensure that one's capital stack remains functional under a range of scenarios.*

Let's examine these dimensions more closely.

Immediacy: The Power of Now

Assets that are high in immediacy can be accessed and liquidated within hours, if not minutes. These include:

Physical cash (in dominant currencies like USD, CHF, SGD)

Stablecoins held in self-custodied wallets (e.g., USDC, DAI)

Highly liquid securities (blue-chip equities, ETFs)

Gold stored in accessible locations or with direct redemption rights

Immediacy is not about long-term yield. It's about *short-term survival and strategic action.* In a liquidity event—such as a bank run, blackout, or capital control—your ability to act decisively depends on how much you can mobilise *without permission.*

However, immediacy often comes at the cost of durability. Fiat cash devalues under inflation. Stablecoins are subject to smart contract risk. Public equities can crash or be halted. This is why immediacy alone is not sufficient—it must be *paired with durability.*

Durability: Surviving Time and Turmoil

Durable assets retain their value over extended periods, often across economic regimes. They act as anchors in a volatile world. These include:

Physical gold and silver (especially held outside the banking system)

Productive land or resource-rich property

Bitcoin (held in cold storage)

Equity in well-governed, cash-generative private businesses

Durability ensures that wealth *persists* even when systems fail. It is less about agility, more about endurance. However, these assets are often harder to liquidate or move, making them vulnerable in high-speed scenarios.

Durability is essential for long-term planning, inheritance, and capital preservation. But without some layer of immediacy, it can become a gilded cage.

Portability: Moving Without Friction

Portability refers to the ability to *relocate wealth without detection, delay, or degradation.* This is where most traditional portfolios fail spectacularly.

Truly portable assets include:

Bitcoin (and other censorship-resistant crypto assets)

High-value bearer assets (e.g., diamonds, certain art, select watches)

Tokenised assets on global blockchains

Intellectual property or digital royalties with global payout rails

A Swiss bank account may be durable and even liquid—but not portable if you're flagged or blocked. A rental property may be income-generative, but try moving it across borders.

Portability is what makes wealth sovereign. It removes geography as a constraint. But highly portable assets often come with volatility or regulatory risk. Hence, *portability is a weapon—but it must be balanced with stability*.

Applying the Triangle: Strategic Allocation Principles

The key insight of the Liquidity Triangle is this: *every asset you hold should justify its position across all three sides*. If it lacks immediacy, you must pair it with something that doesn't. If it lacks durability, ensure its purpose is short-term. If it lacks portability, build parallel channels that can move.

A balanced liquidity triangle might look like this:

Immediacy-heavy: 15–20% of assets in self-custodied stablecoins, cash, or redeemable metals

Durability-heavy: 40–50% in long-term stores (e.g., Bitcoin, gold, quality real estate, private businesses)

Portability-heavy: 30–40% in digital bearer assets, intellectual property, or internationalised capital

This allocation is not prescriptive—but indicative. The ratio shifts based on your risk model, jurisdiction, and time horizon. A Ukrainian entrepreneur in 2022 needed 60% portability. A Singaporean family office in 2025 might prefer 70% durability. *What matters is that each layer reinforces the others, and no single failure collapses your capital function.*

Psychological Liquidity vs. Actual Liquidity

One of the greatest mistakes in wealth management is confusing theoretical access with real access. An investor may *believe* their ETF portfolio is liquid—until trading halts in a crash. A retiree may think their pension is secure—until inflation or reform undermines its value. A founder may assume their business equity is valuable—until political risk renders it unsellable.

Liquidity is not what you think you can do with an asset. It's what you can actually do with it under constraint. Psychological liquidity is a mirage; actual liquidity is tested in pressure.

This is where the liquidity triangle acts not just as a portfolio tool—but as a cognitive discipline. It forces you to question the *function* of each asset in your stack. What is it for? What stress does it withstand? What role does it play when others break?

Friction is the Hidden Cost of Centralisation

Liquidity is not only about markets—it is also about *infrastructure.* Centralised systems impose friction by design. They rely on gatekeepers, banking hours, KYC requirements, jurisdictional compliance. When everything works, this is tolerable. But when systems lock down—whether due to sanctions, censorship, or crisis—friction becomes fatal.

A decentralised liquidity triangle minimises these frictions. It favours:

Peer-to-peer networks over institutional rails

Multisig wallets over custodial platforms

Open protocols over proprietary infrastructure

Global settlement mechanisms over jurisdictional clearing houses

This is not ideological. It is practical. *Every layer of dependency is a potential point of lock-up.*

Final Reflection: Wealth as a Liquid Architecture

To treat wealth as static—assets, holdings, statements—is to misunderstand its nature. *True capital is a liquid architecture.* It is a system of flows, not just stores. It must move through time, across borders, around blocks.

The Liquidity Triangle is not just a framework for portfolios—it is a blueprint for sovereignty. It reminds us that value is not only what we hold, but what we can move *when it matters most.*

In the age of capital controls, digital surveillance, inflationary drift, and geopolitical fracture, liquidity is no longer a convenience. It is a defence. It is freedom disguised as finance.

And when the world closes in, it is the triangle that holds.

Chapter 8
Beyond Borders, Beyond Banking

We find ourselves in an era where the very mechanisms once crafted to provide steadiness have, paradoxically, become the sources of instability. National currencies—historically seen as reliable vessels for preserving value—are today vulnerable to inflationary erosion, invasive surveillance, and the whims of political interference. The banking sector, a cornerstone of financial life for over a century, has drifted from its original role as steward of capital to something far less neutral: a gatekeeper of access. Meanwhile, citizenship—once viewed as a mutually upheld contract between individual and nation—has morphed into a set of unilateral terms, subject to revision without consent.

And yet, even as these foundational institutions degrade, most people remain tethered—almost instinctively—to the geography of their birthright and the legacy infrastructure of a financial order built for a very different century. That loyalty, while understandable, has become not just outdated, but hazardous.

This chapter explores how one might begin to intelligently uncouple from compromised systems—without opting out of civilisation altogether. It's not about ideological rebellion or contrarian flair, but about building a framework of strategic flexibility. For those designing sovereign capital strategies, the motivation isn't novelty or aesthetics. It's something more urgent: resilience, privacy, continuity, and a reclaimed sense of agency.

"Offshore", once a term reserved for shadowy islands and discreet legal arrangements, has evolved into something far more abstract—and powerful. It's no longer a place. It's a mindset. A reconfiguration. A living protocol. Today's approaches to asset protection and financial mobility have little to do with secret vaults or exotic jurisdictions. They lie in encrypted ledgers, decentralised identifiers, cross-border property portfolios, and income that flows without a postcode. The sovereign individual, once a hypothetical ideal, has become a working model—quietly adopted by builders, thinkers, and operators across the globe.

This chapter rests on three central assertions. First, that the traditional banking system—particularly in jurisdictions heavy with regulation—can no longer serve those who aim to operate independently. Second, that where one lives, and what one owns there, must now be assessed not merely in terms of comfort or returns, but as strategic infrastructure. Third, that real resilience no longer lives solely in the individual—it lives in the network. Without trusted nodes of support scattered across borders, no one can truly be prepared.

Let's begin by confronting a familiar illusion: the so-called "offshore account". For decades, the phrase conjured images of discretion, prestige, or clever tax positioning. But the last twenty years—sped along by frameworks like FATCA, CRS, and a swelling tide of anti-money laundering compliance—have turned that fantasy inside out. Today, traditional offshore arrangements are less private, more surveilled, and increasingly reserved for the ultra-wealthy. The cliché of tucking money away in the Caymans or Jersey? It's not just outdated—it's misleading.

In its place, a new financial paradigm has emerged. Decentralised, programmable, borderless. Systems like Bitcoin, Monero, Ethereum, and their various layer-2 expansions now offer the ability to transfer value directly, manage reserves without intermediaries, and settle transactions immune to censorship—all without requiring SWIFT codes, IBANs, or legacy bank infrastructure. Stablecoins, when held with care, provide access to dollar liquidity without touching a traditional bank at all. In this world, "offshore" isn't where your wealth resides. It's how your systems are configured.

But digital sophistication alone cannot safeguard the sovereign individual. One can have the most elegant, decentralised financial architecture imaginable—and still find themselves exposed if their physical freedom is confined within the borders of a faltering regime. This brings us to the second pillar of the chapter: real estate, not merely as investment, but as exit infrastructure. Increasingly, individuals are abandoning the assumption that home should mean a singular, permanent base. Instead, they are assembling geographies of possibility: a Lisbon flat. A Georgian cottage. A parcel in Uruguay. These are not escapist fantasies—they are continuity plans.

This isn't about luxury, either. It's about redundancy. In a world where property rights are local—but risk is indisputably global—having a single point of failure is no longer prudent. Multi-location living is no longer indulgence. It's strategy. "Home" has ceased to be a matter of sentiment alone. It's become the fallback.

Still, property—like capital—can only go so far. In moments of uncertainty, it is the people around you who determine whether you can move, adapt, survive. In an environment of shrinking trust and rising digital scrutiny, social capital has quietly become the most vital and undervalued asset. Encrypted chat groups. Loosely organised alliances. Private masterminds. Networks of mobile, like-minded professionals. These groups now function much like extended families or religious congregations once did—only faster, more agile, and often, more aligned in action. They co-locate, co-invest, co-evacuate. In a world filled with synthetic connections and algorithmic manipulation, real community is not a luxury. It is infrastructure.

Over the following pages, we will examine each of these elements in detail. You will see why decentralised finance is steadily eclipsing traditional offshore methods—not only in functionality, but in moral coherence. You will explore how to choose and maintain properties across multiple jurisdictions, not simply for appreciation, but for presence and safety. And you will come to understand what it truly takes to build meaningful, transnational networks—ones that don't merely connect, but respond.

We'll challenge the notion that sovereignty equates to isolation. If anything, it's the opposite. True sovereignty is about integrating intelligently into ecosystems without becoming beholden to any one of them. We'll explore regulatory arbitrage, nomadic residency programmes, decentralised identity structures, and the ethical obligations of operating outside the usual lanes.

Make no mistake: this is not a wistful endorsement of disappearance. This chapter is not about running away. It's about meeting the world on terms you've consciously chosen. Sovereignty, in the years ahead, won't be defined by escape—it will be shaped by configuration. To live across borders is not to renounce the state, the bank, or the idea of home. It is to ensure that none of them alone can capture or define you.

By the time we conclude, you will not only have a roadmap for moving assets, establishing footholds, and deepening your relationships beyond the grasp of brittle systems. You will also understand why doing so is no longer an edge—it's a necessity.

Because the storm will come. Of that, there is little doubt. And when it does, those who have prepared—quietly, deliberately—will not be scrambling. They will be building. Thriving. Ready for whatever comes next.

The Stateless Investor – Exploring Second Passports and New Identity Strategies

For most of human history, identity has been inseparable from territory. One's rights, obligations, and social standing were dictated by the state—or tribe—one was born into. This territoriality became codified in the Westphalian model of statehood and reinforced by the industrial-era assumption that productivity, citizenship, and residency should all be confined to the same geography. Today, however, that model is quietly unravelling.

In a world where capital moves faster than laws can regulate, where digital nomadism has decoupled labour from location, and where political instability is not limited to the "developing world," the conventional passport has become less of a privilege and more of a bottleneck. For many, it is a source of restriction rather than freedom. It is within this context that the **stateless investor** emerges—not as a utopian idealist, but as a pragmatic strategist: one who understands that sovereignty begins with the capacity to choose *where you belong and on what terms.*

Second citizenship is no longer a luxury reserved for the ultra-wealthy or fringe survivalists. It is fast becoming a core asset class in the portfolios of globally minded professionals, entrepreneurs, and those building generational wealth. This chapter explores how identity itself can be restructured—not abandoned, but *optimised*—through legal, ethical, and strategically sound frameworks.

Identity as a Constraint

Let's begin with a blunt reality: most people are prisoners of their passports. A single citizenship often determines the tax regimes you're subject to, the jurisdictions where you may own property or start companies, and the currencies you're expected to earn and spend. It defines your exposure to surveillance, capital controls, conscription, exit taxes, travel restrictions, and—crucially—your *dependency on a single legal ecosystem.*

For Americans, for example, citizenship is a global liability. The United States imposes taxation on worldwide income regardless of residency. Citizens must disclose foreign bank accounts, report international holdings, and navigate labyrinthine compliance regimes like FATCA and FBAR. For others, such as citizens of Venezuela, Afghanistan, or even post-Brexit Britain, the issue is less tax and more access: travel restrictions, collapsing currency systems, and geopolitical stigma turn the passport from an instrument of mobility into a symbol of fragility.

The solution isn't to reject nationality—it's to diversify it.

The Rise of the Multipassport Mindset

Much like investors distribute capital across uncorrelated assets to mitigate risk, sovereign individuals are diversifying identity across jurisdictions. A second (or third) citizenship acts not only as a hedge against political risk but as a *gateway to opportunity*. It can unlock visa-free travel, legal residency in stable countries, new business environments, and access to better educational or medical systems.

There are broadly three strategies for acquiring secondary citizenship, each with its trade-offs:

1. **Citizenship by Descent**: Many countries—such as Ireland, Italy, Poland, and Israel—offer citizenship to individuals with ancestral ties. This route is often underutilised despite being cost-effective and relatively fast, especially for those with European lineage. The primary limitation is bureaucratic: applicants must navigate archival records, language barriers, and documentation standards set decades ago.

2. **Citizenship by Naturalisation**: This is the traditional path—reside in a country legally for a number of years, integrate culturally, and apply. Portugal, Uruguay, and Georgia are examples of countries offering relatively friendly naturalisation pathways, especially to entrepreneurs, remote workers, and investors. However, naturalisation demands a long-term commitment and offers no immediate protections during the waiting period.

3. **Citizenship by Investment (CBI)**: More controversial but increasingly common, CBI programmes allow individuals to acquire passports by making significant financial contributions—either through real estate, government bonds, or direct donations. Countries like St. Kitts & Nevis, Dominica, Antigua, and Malta offer varying packages. While critics view these as commodifications of national identity, proponents argue they are simply a modern expression of capital meritocracy: if you can contribute meaningfully to a state, why shouldn't you be allowed access?

What's vital is not just acquiring multiple nationalities, but *structuring them intelligently*. A redundant passport is not inherently valuable. What matters is how *complementary* they are. A Grenadian passport, for instance, offers visa-free access to China, whereas most European documents do not. A Turkish passport allows rapid E2 visa access to the United States—something unavailable to citizens of India or South Africa. The goal is not passport collection—it's functional flexibility.

Statelessness and Legal Identity in the Digital Age

Now consider the concept at the frontier of this evolution: *constructive statelessness*. This doesn't mean giving up all national ties—nor is it legally advisable in most cases—but rather, *decoupling your essential functions from any one government's oversight*. This is increasingly feasible as identity becomes digitised and decentralised.

Today, self-sovereign identity (SSI) technologies allow individuals to authenticate themselves, sign contracts, and verify credentials without relying on centralised databases. Projects such as Estonia's e-Residency or decentralised ID systems like ION or Veramo are paving the way for non-jurisdictional proof of identity—meaning you can work, bank, and transact globally while keeping your legal "centre of gravity" deliberately diffuse.

Such configurations are not purely technical—they are legal strategies. A stateless investor might, for instance, combine:

A tax residency in a territorial-tax country (e.g., Panama or UAE)

Citizenship in a visa-friendly jurisdiction (e.g., Malta or Dominica)

A business registered in a flexible common law entity (e.g., Nevis LLC or Singapore Pte Ltd)

Digital identity credentials issued via SSI protocols (enabling secure sign-in, employment, and governance)

This layered identity model allows individuals to function across domains without being wholly dependent on any one. *Resilience is no longer about having a single strong passport—it's about having interoperable ones.*

Ethical Considerations and Misuse

Of course, the rise of stateless investing raises ethical and legal questions. Is this merely elite arbitrage? Are we creating a two-tiered system where only the wealthy can opt out of broken states? Will sovereign individuals be held to account if they operate outside the reach of enforcement?

These are valid concerns, but they assume the status quo is just and universal. In truth, *many who pursue sovereign identity strategies are not the rich fleeing taxes—but the globally mobile seeking fairness, privacy, and continuity*. Moreover, it is not the legal structure itself that creates inequality, but access to tools and knowledge. Democratising these strategies—through education, open legal frameworks, and civic-minded design—is part of the solution.

The Future of Identity Is Configurable

The nation-state will not vanish overnight. Passports will continue to matter. But the rise of the stateless investor signals a broader shift: *identity is becoming modular*. Where you are born will matter less than how you configure your affiliations, contracts, and presence in the world.

This chapter does not advocate recklessness. It advocates awareness. If your identity is your ultimate point of leverage, *you should manage it with the same rigour you apply to capital*. Second citizenships, digital IDs, e-residencies, and decentralised authentication protocols are not indulgences—they are tools for continuity in a fractured world.

The Stateless Investor is not escaping responsibility. They are *engineering autonomy*.

And as the geopolitical landscape grows more volatile, the question will not be who you belong to—but *who belongs to you*.

The Offshore is Now Online – Debunking Myths About Offshore Banking and Highlighting Digital Alternatives

Offshore banking has long been the cinematic shorthand for secrecy, scandal, and escape. It conjures images of Caribbean vaults, shell corporations hidden behind brass plaques, and anonymous transfers made in tropical twilight. But that portrayal—equal parts myth and melodrama—now belongs to a dying world. The real transformation, and the real story worth telling, is not about physical islands, but digital infrastructures. The offshore of the 21st century isn't a place you fly to. It's a network you log into.

The offshore is no longer about geography—it's about jurisdictional leverage, data custody, and programmable finance. And its most powerful tools today are digital, decentralised, and often legally transparent. This shift is not just semantic; it's structural. For those building resilient, border-agnostic portfolios, understanding how the offshore has evolved—and what it now enables—is essential. Not to hide, but to endure.

The Fiction of Secrecy and the Reality of Strategy

Popular media still frames offshore banking as inherently illicit: a realm for tax cheats, oligarchs, and international criminals. This misrepresentation serves two purposes. First, it flatters domestic banking monopolies by implying that any exit is suspicious. Second, it distracts from the reality that offshore banking has long been a lifeline for those escaping capital controls, authoritarian regimes, inflationary meltdowns, and confiscatory policies.

To be clear, offshore banking—when pursued transparently and in compliance with the law—is entirely legitimate. For millions of individuals worldwide, it is not about evasion; it's about *preservation.* And as the traditional offshore jurisdictions have come under pressure from global regulatory initiatives—FATCA, CRS, OECD blacklists—savvy asset holders are no longer seeking secrecy. They're seeking *strategic distance.*

This is where the online offshore begins.

From Vaults to Protocols: The Rise of Digital Custody

At the core of this transformation is the dematerialisation of assets. What once required bricks, safes, and private banks now exists as lines of code and encrypted ledgers. Capital can be held in multi-signature wallets, governed by smart contracts, or even streamed in real-time using programmable finance rails.

The implications are profound. Instead of parking wealth in Swiss numbered accounts, today's sovereign individual might:

Hold stablecoins in a decentralised wallet with no custodial counterparty

Operate through a digital foundation domiciled in a favourable jurisdiction

Stream income via blockchain-based smart contracts that disburse according to pre-set rules

Obscure not through opacity, but through architectural redundancy—diversifying across jurisdictions, protocols, and legal entities

This is not about hiding. It's about removing single points of failure. The goal is not to be invisible, but *uninterruptible.*

Decentralised finance (DeFi) platforms now offer services once monopolised by private banks: savings instruments, collateralised loans, yield-bearing vaults, even synthetic equities. With appropriate legal wrappers and tax compliance, these can function as the modern offshore—not shady, but *sovereign-aware.*

Jurisdiction Without Geography

One of the most powerful insights of modern finance is that *jurisdiction and geography are decoupling.* Where your assets are *held* is no longer where they are *accessed.* A trust registered in Nevis might own a company in Singapore that controls a multi-currency wallet interfacing with decentralised apps globally.

Each of these nodes—trust, company, wallet—can be in distinct regulatory ecosystems, yet operate harmoniously. The old offshore world depended on secrecy and access barriers. The new model relies on *architecture and interoperability.*

Consider the emergence of **e-residency programmes**. Estonia's e-Residency has enabled over 100,000 entrepreneurs to register EU-based companies, access international banking, and operate remotely—all without ever setting foot in the country. This is a legal offshore strategy that is both *transparent and scalable.* The critical shift? Residency, banking, and identity are no longer assumed to live in the same nation-state.

Digital identity solutions, including self-sovereign identity protocols (SSI), are further dissolving old assumptions. With SSI, individuals can sign contracts, access services, and verify their credentials *without a centralised database.* This is not theory. It's already being piloted across Europe, Latin America, and Asia.

The offshore, once a physical redoubt, is becoming a modular configuration of rights and access across systems.

Challenging the Monopoly of Domestic Custodians

One of the most insidious myths propagated by traditional financial systems is that safety lies in compliance with a single domestic framework. But what happens when that framework itself becomes predatory, erratic, or unstable?

History offers too many examples to ignore:

Cyprus (2013): Bank bail-ins led to the seizure of uninsured deposits above €100,000

Argentina (multiple periods): Capital controls and hyperinflation wiped out savings overnight

Lebanon (2019–): Frozen accounts and strict withdrawal limits rendered citizens financially paralysed

Nigeria (2021–): Crackdowns on crypto usage and deteriorating currency stability closed off alternative escape routes

In each case, the problem wasn't criminal behaviour by depositors—it was a structural fragility in the domestic system. By contrast, *offshore digital alternatives provide individuals with functional autonomy, even under adverse conditions.* Whether through jurisdictional diversity or decentralised protocols, the principle is the same: *no single entity should be able to freeze, seize, or surveil your assets without recourse.*

The offshore is no longer about evading responsibility. It is about *reclaiming agency.*

Compliance Isn't the Opposite of Sovereignty

A common strawman is that all offshore strategies are about dodging taxes. In reality, the new generation of digital offshore thinkers is often *hyper-compliant.* They structure their affairs with legal counsel, file appropriate disclosures, and design architectures that are not dependent on secrecy.

What they reject is not law—but monopoly. The idea that only domestic banks, operating under one regulatory regime, should control your financial fate is both anachronistic and dangerous. What they embrace is *selective exposure*—choosing where, how, and under what terms they interact with financial infrastructure.

And increasingly, those terms are *programmable.* One can now design wallets that require multiple signers, that release funds on the basis of verified actions, or that interact only with pre-approved contracts. This is not financial opacity—it is *financial autonomy by design.*

The Future of the Offshore is Infrastructure, Not Islands

Looking ahead, the most influential offshore banks will not be banks at all. They will be protocols, platforms, and hybrid entities that combine legal clarity with technological robustness.

Expect to see:

Jurisdictional DAOs (Decentralised Autonomous Organisations) that offer cross-border asset custody with governance baked into code

Digital foundations operating on public blockchains with embedded auditability

Tokenised real-world assets (RWAs) that can be held, traded, and collateralised globally, yet still recognised under legal frameworks

Integration between decentralised finance (DeFi) platforms and compliant identity verification (e.g. zk-KYC), enabling lawful privacy

This convergence means that future offshore strategies will be not only more resilient, but more *visible to those who matter*—regulators, partners, beneficiaries—*and invisible to those who don't.*

Why This Matters Now

We are entering an era of financial tightening, increasing geopolitical uncertainty, and aggressive digitisation of state power. Central bank digital currencies (CBDCs) will offer convenience—but at the cost of programmability by the state. Access to international transfers may be tied to "trusted" citizenships. Wealth may become harder to move, harder to shield, and easier to scrutinise.

In this climate, *the offshore must be reframed*—not as a loophole, but as a necessity. Not as an indulgence, but as infrastructure. The question for thoughtful investors is no longer "should I go offshore?" but "how can I construct my digital and legal presence to withstand disruption without sacrificing compliance?"

The answer is not found in secrecy. It is found in design.

Homes Without Countries – Rethinking Real Estate as Protection When Nations Turn Unstable

For centuries, real estate has been considered the quintessential safe asset. It's physical, tangible, and perceived as inherently stable. But that assumption is increasingly misaligned with geopolitical reality. A home may be built of stone, but its fate rests on the soil beneath it—and more crucially, on the legal, financial, and political system that claims jurisdiction over that soil. When nations falter, collapse, or become hostile to private capital, property is not protected by bricks—it is exposed by borders.

The future of resilient ownership does not lie in physical immovability, but in legal and operational mobility. The idea of a home tied immutably to a single flag is being challenged by investors, dissidents, and mobile professionals alike. What is emerging in its place is a new philosophy of asset shelter: *homes without countries.* Not stateless in law, but *unanchored in dependency.* A real estate strategy built not for growth alone, but for *escape, resilience, and optionality.*

The Illusion of Domestic Safety

Western investors, particularly in historically stable democracies, often assume their home-country property is immune to risk. But property is only as secure as the rule of law that upholds title, enforces contract, and deters confiscation. And these pillars are not permanent—they are *political artefacts*, vulnerable to erosion.

Consider the following:

Cyprus, 2013: In the wake of a banking collapse, property-owning foreigners were disproportionately targeted for capital levies and asset freezes.

Zimbabwe, 2000s: Legal title held no weight once land reform policies reclassified private farms as "reclaimable" by the state.

Turkey, 2020s: Real estate belonging to critics of the regime—journalists, academics, NGOs—was seized under emergency laws.

Canada, 2022: Protesters found their bank accounts and financial assets frozen without trial, revealing how dissent can translate into sudden asset risk, even in developed democracies.

These are not edge cases. They are reminders that *legal ownership is not absolute—it is contingent.* When economic stress intensifies or political systems centralise, property becomes an easy target for control.

Real estate is visible, local, and taxable. And those three features make it vulnerable, not secure, when things begin to unravel.

Physical Immutability vs. Strategic Optionality

Traditional real estate portfolios tend to be concentrated in one's home country, often near one's main residence. This concentration is rational under conditions of long-term national stability, predictable property rights, and moderate tax regimes. But it becomes a liability when any of those variables change. A real estate portfolio confined to one jurisdiction is an *unhedged bet on that nation's future.*

By contrast, global real estate strategies that span legal jurisdictions, political regimes, and economic environments provide *escape routes, income buffers, and diplomatic leverage.* The strategic investor is not looking for maximum yield, but for *asymmetric protection*—the kind that matters most when domestic systems fail.

And increasingly, this does not mean building a mansion in Switzerland. It may mean holding a small, energy-autonomous home in rural Portugal, a serviced apartment in Georgia (Tbilisi), or a citizenship-eligible property in Vanuatu. What matters is not prestige—it's *mobility, functionality, and legal flexibility.*

Asset protection in an age of sovereign volatility is not about hiding—it is about positioning.

Property as Plan B: Global Ownership as Escape Valve

The phrase "second passport" is often understood in legal terms—another nationality, another travel document. But *real estate can be a passport of its own.* Not just to residency programmes or citizenship-by-investment schemes, but to *exit.* A bolthole. A base of operations. A pre-positioned fallback.

Examples:

Chile and Uruguay have become safe havens for North Americans seeking real estate with water rights, arable land, and minimal geopolitical exposure.

Thailand offers long-term elite visas tied to property ownership, providing flexibility without a full citizenship path.

Portugal's Golden Visa—until recently tied to real estate—enabled thousands to gain European mobility through modest property investments, many under €500,000.

These structures may be under political pressure, but they reflect a deeper logic: *property abroad can secure rights of residence, economic footholds, and diplomatic latitude.* For individuals whose domestic regimes become hostile—due to wealth, politics, or ethnicity—this can be life-saving.

Ownership vs. Control: Structuring Beyond Borders

Owning a home abroad is not the same as being protected by it. The key lies in *how it is held.* Structuring matters—deeply.

A property held in your personal name, in a country where your primary government has reach (via treaties, banking surveillance, or mutual enforcement), is not meaningfully offshore. If it can be frozen by your home authorities, seized in a divorce, or tied up in probate, it *is not resilient.*

By contrast, holding property through *foreign entities, irrevocable trusts, or limited liability structures*—ideally in jurisdictions that do not recognise foreign judgments—adds legal insulation. These aren't tricks; they're risk-adjusted mechanisms. And when paired with second residency or alternative banking setups, they create a holistic system of protection.

This is where many fail. They buy abroad, but they structure domestically. The true philosophy of homes without countries requires both *location independence* and *custodial autonomy.*

Rental Markets, Not Refuge: The Rise of Globally Fluid Living

There is also a generational shift in how real estate is perceived. Younger professionals, location-independent entrepreneurs, and digital nomads are less interested in property as a symbol of permanence. Instead, they see real estate as *access*, not ownership. This shift has birthed entirely new asset strategies.

Examples include:

Investing in short-term rental properties across regulatory grey zones where foreign ownership is allowed but lightly taxed—e.g., Mexico, Albania, Montenegro.

Fractional ownership of villas or serviced apartments that provide usable nights, citizenship eligibility, and capital appreciation, without full managerial burden.

Tokenised real estate platforms, allowing access to real estate-backed yields with instant liquidity—no title transfers, no border crossings.

These models reflect a mindset shift: *real estate can be a function of optionality rather than legacy*. It can be about *accessing freedom*, not accumulating status.

Ethical Considerations: Responsibility in Global Footprints

Of course, there are valid critiques of globalised real estate strategies. In some cities, foreign buying has inflated prices, displaced locals, and commodified basic shelter. This raises critical ethical questions: *How can global investors participate without undermining local resilience?*

A thoughtful investor should consider:

Supporting local economies through partnerships, not extraction

Choosing regions actively seeking foreign investment as part of national policy (e.g., post-crisis zones offering incentives)

Structuring properties for income or productivity, not idle speculation

Resilience without exploitation is possible. But it requires conscious structuring, not opportunistic accumulation.

Real Estate as Signal and Shield

Ultimately, property sends signals. To states. To tax authorities. To regulators. It is visible, recordable, and accessible. In turbulent times, this makes it both a *risk* and a *negotiating asset.*

A well-placed property can offer diplomatic cover: you pay local taxes, contribute to the economy, and thereby build goodwill. It can also act as a *humanitarian lifeline*—offering not just legal escape, but physical refuge.

But this requires foresight. If you wait until your home country imposes exit taxes, seizes foreign income, or collapses into conflict, *it is too late.* The philosophy of homes without countries is not reactionary—it is preemptive.

In a world where borders are weaponised, laws are politicised, and capital is monitored, homes must evolve from static symbols of permanence into mobile frameworks of freedom. The strongest shelter is not the thickest wall, but the widest access. Real estate, thoughtfully acquired, ethically held, and jurisdictionally diversified, remains a potent form of protection.

Just not in the ways we were taught to believe.

Building a Global Support Network – Encrypted Groups and Trust-Based Communities as the New Havens

In times of political fracture, institutional decay, and global fragmentation, wealth alone does not equate to safety. Nor does knowledge, unless it is embedded in a network capable of responding with speed and cohesion. Increasingly, it is not the assets in your portfolio but the *people in your encrypted channels*—the ones who know you, trust you, and can mobilise when institutions freeze—that determine whether you can act swiftly, decisively, and with protection.

The most powerful asset class in a destabilising world is not digital currency, real estate, or legal entities—it is *high-trust, decentralised human capital.* Not bureaucracies. Not alliances. *Networks.* And not networks in the abstract, but specific, curated, strategic communities that cross borders, share asymmetric information, and function with resilience when central systems falter.

This is not utopianism. It is the hard-won lesson of dissidents, war-zone operators, and financial nomads: *you are only as secure as the people who can vouch for you when the lights go out.*

Why Traditional Institutions Fail in Crisis

Banks, courts, governments, and even NGOs are structured for normalcy. They function well under routine stress. But when systems come under systemic pressure—war, censorship, financial collapse—these institutions become brittle. They obey hierarchy, not context. They follow protocol, not nuance. They protect policy, not people.

Case in point: during the 2022 invasion of Ukraine, international banking systems failed to protect ordinary civilians. SWIFT access was revoked. Card networks broke down. Refugees—doctors, engineers, entrepreneurs—fled across borders only to find their entire digital footprint deemed suspect. In that context, a single Telegram group with 50 trusted contacts willing to offer lodging, make crypto payments, or activate legal contacts proved more effective than state-level support.

That was not a one-off. Similar decentralised resilience played out during the fall of Kabul, the Hong Kong protests, and the lockdowns in Shanghai. State actors couldn't respond fast enough. Platforms couldn't arbitrate trust. It was *networks that moved people and resources with precision.*

The Anatomy of a Resilient Network

A resilient support network is not simply a friend group or social media following. It is a deliberately cultivated structure, governed by three essential traits:

1. **Trust, not scale**: The strength of a resilient network is not measured by size but by *integrity of trust.* Every added member increases potential attack surface—technical, reputational, legal. Real protection comes from *low entropy, high alignment* groups where signal is high and noise is filtered out.

2. **Encryption as infrastructure**: End-to-end encryption is not a lifestyle choice—it is a *requirement* for operational freedom. Signal, Matrix, Session, and decentralised key-sharing protocols (like those used in Web3 DAOs) form the backbone of modern protection. The best support networks *cannot be surveilled because they do not centralise data.*

3. **Actionable roles, not passive presence**: Membership in a resilient group comes with implicit capability. Who can wire stablecoins on short notice? Who has legal contacts in offshore

jurisdictions? Who can offer emergency housing? If your group is only theoretical, it won't activate when it matters. *Everyone in a robust network knows what they're for.*

The strongest modern networks operate like asymmetric teams—not democratic forums. Trust is earned through reliability and reciprocity, not charisma or branding. Members are selected, not accepted.

Encryption is the New Border

Encrypted infrastructure is more than privacy—it is *territory*. A high-trust network housed in Signal, coordinated through Matrix, and hardened with private keys offers *jurisdictional insulation.* States can coerce platforms, subpoena ISPs, or freeze cloud accounts. But they cannot decrypt what was never exposed.

This is not merely a concern for journalists or political activists. Wealth holders, entrepreneurs, and cross-border families are now regular targets for overreach—from sudden capital controls to retroactive taxation, algorithmic flagging of transactions, and surveillance-based profiling.

In this context, platforms like:

ProtonMail (Switzerland) for secure communications

Keybase or Session for identity-resistant channels

Tails OS and Qubes OS for hardware-secure coordination

Monero or ZCash for privacy-preserving financial flows

… are no longer fringe tools. They are the operational layer of *networked sovereignty*. The encryption stack is now part of the *sovereign portfolio*—just as essential as gold or crypto.

Network Effects vs. Trust Density

It's tempting to equate network size with power. But in resilience, *density matters more than reach.* A Telegram group of 20 people who've met in real life, share mission alignment, and have rehearsed fallback plans is worth more than 20,000 Twitter followers.

In practical terms, building a high-density network means:

Meeting offline when possible to establish identity verification

Sharing legal jurisdictions and financial tools to align risk strategies

Maintaining redundancies in communications—if Signal is down, where do we reconvene?

This is especially critical in exfiltration scenarios: when someone needs to flee a collapsing regime, liquidate assets under duress, or disappear from state surveillance. In these moments, trust density determines *speed of activation* and *survivability.*

Community as Currency

In historical contexts, diasporas have long operated this way. Jewish, Armenian, and Lebanese communities have demonstrated for generations that *networks outperform institutions under persecution.* The mechanisms were analogue: letters of credit, familial houses, merchant relationships.

Today, the same principles apply—but with cryptographic precision and global scalability.

When financial tools become programmable, *the trust-based community becomes a programmable bank.* Smart contracts can allocate emergency funds via multi-signature wallets. Time-locked transactions can activate based on GPS coordinates or biometric keys. *The community becomes not just a source of advice, but a node of execution.*

This changes the relationship between individual and system. You no longer rely on a bank manager's goodwill or a bureaucrat's interpretation of your legal rights. You rely on *code, trust, and readiness.*

Fragility of Identity, Power of Belonging

Ironically, as borders harden, passports proliferate, and digital IDs expand, the core unit of security is shrinking. It's not the nation-state. It's not the megacorp. It's the *trusted pod.* Your pod is the handful of people who can find you when you go dark. Who know your operational alias. Who can vouch for you under another identity.

Building this kind of relationship requires more than networking—it requires *reputation architecture.* Over time, individuals who consistently deliver, stay silent when needed, and offer value without asking for applause build relational equity that no bank can issue and no court can replicate.

In the end, the most valuable thing you can possess may not be an offshore account or a second passport—but *a dozen people who'd take a risk for you because you've taken risks for them.*

The Practical Path Forward

To build your global support network:

1. **Start small and be selective**: Quality over quantity. Curate relationships based on shared principles, operational competence, and discretion.

2. **Invest in overlapping tools**: Learn the tech stack. Not just how to send crypto or use Signal—but how to do it *under pressure.*

3. **Share the load**: Mutualise knowledge. Designate roles. Build playbooks. If one goes down, the others know what to do.

4. **Align legally and ethically**: Don't build black-market enclaves. Build resilient communities that function *within the bounds of law*—but beyond the reach of bad law.

This isn't an abstract theory. It's already happening in corners of the world most people ignore—cooperative DAOs, crypto co-living experiments, underground mentoring networks, mutual aid circles for political dissidents, and sovereign technology guilds.

They're not waiting for institutional permission. They're building havens from the ground up. Quietly. Securely. Effectively.

In the coming years, the greatest risk will not be lack of money, but lack of trust. In that world, a well-forged encrypted community is not just a backup—it is a primary line of defence.

You don't need a million followers. You need twelve people who will pick up when it matters.

And you need to be one of them, too.

Chapter 9
The Ethics of Escape

There's always been something morally charged about the act of withdrawing from broken systems. When an individual decides to step beyond the boundaries of conventional structures—financial, territorial, or ideological—they're not just making a practical adjustment. They are, whether consciously or not, making a statement. In an age where institutional overreach has become the norm, where the interests of state and corporation bleed into each other, and where surveillance is sold as seamless convenience, choosing autonomy is easily mistaken for extremism. But as these systems grow more extractive and less accountable, a difficult question arises: is it still ethical to comply with machinery that no longer serves the common good?

This chapter doesn't traffic in easy reassurances. Nor does it suggest that stepping away from the mainstream is somehow neutral. The moment you engage in decentralised finance, hedge your assets against inflationary decay, or move across borders with encrypted contingencies, you cross a threshold. You're not vanishing—you're reassigning responsibility. You're shifting allegiance—from imposed frameworks to your own principles, your loved ones, and the horizon ahead.

What underpins this shift is a quiet yet profound philosophical tension—one that cuts across psychology, society, and ethics. We'll work through that tension in three sections. First, we'll probe the narrow divide between caution and paranoia, between protection and a fortress mentality. The growing accessibility of privacy tools invites their responsible use—but not obsession. Building resilience doesn't mean disappearing. It means knowing what to shield, from whom, and to what extent—then stopping before your life becomes a bunker.

Next, we'll confront the notion of financial civil disobedience. Not as melodrama, but as a logical answer to malfunctioning systems. When central banks silently devalue savings, when tax structures drift ever further from fair representation, and when compliance props up dysfunction, it becomes worth asking: what obligation remains? What is owed to an order that has defaulted on its promises while demanding unwavering compliance? At what point does staying inside the system become ethically suspect?

Finally, this chapter turns to stewardship. In recent years, the impulse to accumulate—to stash coins, stockpile properties, scatter wealth across jurisdictions—has been understandable. But it's not sufficient. Security, while necessary, is only part of the picture. Wealth without wisdom turns brittle. The true purpose is continuity: to construct frameworks, both tangible and philosophical, that uphold not just your freedom but that of those who'll inherit your world. A well-constructed exit is not an escape plan—it's the scaffolding of legacy.

This reframing matters. All too often, discussions around financial sovereignty collapse into caricature. On one side, the docile citizen who equates privacy with suspicion; on the other, the jittery hoarder convinced that every institution is out to confiscate or collapse. But there's another posture—less theatrical, more mature—that this chapter holds up: that of the steward. Informed, purposeful, and quietly resolute. Not just free, but grounded.

To make these ideas real, we'll turn to lived experience. We'll examine the psychological burden of living in high-surveillance states, where even ordinary transactions carry the weight of potential accusation. We'll revisit moments in history when departure was the only moral path—from the Berliners who scaled walls to Argentinians who saw their wealth evaporate overnight. And we'll consider the present—how technology has enabled subtle, scalable exits: multisig wallets, decentralised earnings, second passports, encrypted messaging channels, and migratory lifestyles tailored for resilience.

But this chapter doesn't pretend to be merely technical. It's a meditation on morality. The Ethics of Escape begins with a recognition: that choosing to shield oneself from deteriorating systems is not a consequence-free act. There are reverberations—social, ethical, familial—and they deserve honest reckoning. When you unplug from something broken, you must ask not only what you're leaving behind—but what you're choosing to build in its place.

Done well, financial escape is neither frantic nor cynical. It's measured. It's principled. It rejects helplessness and embraces stewardship. It doesn't isolate—it equips and informs. This chapter isn't about asset checklists or crypto wallets alone. It's a call to a deeper reckoning: How does one maintain ethical clarity while manoeuvring through systems that, at times, seem designed to erode it?

Escape, when carried out with clarity and care, is not surrender. It is a form of assertion. It tells the truth—not through rhetoric, but through action—about what matters enough to safeguard, and what no longer deserves one's loyalty. It is not disappearance. It is declaration. If the last century taught us to obey central authority, perhaps this one will reward those who choose decentralised integrity—those who leave not in haste, but with intention. Those who exit—not out of fear, but out of conviction.

Is Protection Selfish? – Engaging with the Moral Dilemma of Preparing While Others Suffer

There is a quiet discomfort that shadows the pursuit of personal security. It's rarely spoken aloud, but it nags at thoughtful minds: *Is it ethical to safeguard one's own future when so many others are left exposed?* In a world increasingly defined by asymmetries—of power, of access, of resilience—the act of preparation can begin to look, to some, like a retreat from solidarity. The question is not whether protecting oneself is practical. That much is obvious. The deeper question—moral, psychological, social—is whether such protection is inherently selfish. And if not inherently, then *when* and *why* does it become so?

To understand this tension, one must begin by confronting the false binary at its core. The narrative that pits individual preparedness against collective responsibility is deeply flawed. It assumes that self-protection is necessarily exclusionary—that building a life raft implies indifference to those still in the water. In reality, *resilience and responsibility are not opposites; they are prerequisites to one another.* One cannot meaningfully support others if one is chronically exposed, depleted, or dependent. Preparation, in this sense, becomes the *foundation* for contribution, not the abdication of it.

But this does not exempt the prepared from scrutiny. It is possible—easy, in fact—to cross the line from self-protection into isolationism. The hoarder who withdraws behind steel gates, the speculator who profits off collapse, the digital nomad who avoids every jurisdictional duty but expects the protection of every border they cross—these figures are not fictional. They reflect real decisions with real consequences. The question is how to distinguish *responsible resilience* from *strategic abandonment.* And here, moral clarity demands more than good intentions. It demands a *principled framework* for action.

One productive lens comes from psychology. Research into crisis behaviour reveals that people's capacity to help others is directly correlated with their own sense of agency. In moments of chaos, those who feel powerless tend to narrow their focus: survival for themselves and those closest to them. Conversely, those who feel prepared—emotionally, logistically, structurally—are more likely to reach outward. They are the ones who volunteer in disasters, who share scarce resources, who organise escape routes not just for themselves but for others. *Preparation, then, is not a withdrawal—it is an enabler of ethical action.* The moral question becomes not "Have you protected yourself?" but "What does your protection *allow* you to do for others?"

This is particularly relevant in the context of financial sovereignty. When an individual diversifies assets across jurisdictions, secures non-custodial digital wallets, and builds income streams that cannot be politically throttled, they are not simply insulating themselves from institutional failure. They are also creating optionality—for dependents, for partners, for communities. They become the kind of person others turn to when systems break, not just the kind who survives in silence. *To the extent that personal resilience is quietly transferrable, it ceases to be selfish and becomes service.*

Yet there are real tensions that must not be glossed over. Consider the optics: when elites move assets offshore, acquire second passports, or shift real estate into strategically neutral zones, the perception from the outside is often one of evasion. And this perception is not always wrong. Asset protection can function as ethical cover for asset flight. The line between stewardship and escape is thin—and the difference often lies not in what one does, but *why* and *how* one does it. An offshore structure that shields wealth from authoritarian seizure may be defensible. One that exists solely to dodge taxation in a functioning democracy demands deeper scrutiny.

Here, we enter the terrain of *financial civil ethics*. What are we morally obligated to share with systems we no longer trust? What happens when the rule of law becomes selectively applied, or when economic policies disproportionately punish prudence? At what point does withdrawal become not just understandable, but *just*? These are not questions with binary answers. They require context: the nature of the system, the role of the individual within it, the availability of legal redress, and the visibility of one's exit strategy. It is entirely possible to act in self-defence without undermining the commons. But it requires deliberate thought—and a willingness to interrogate one's own motives.

Philosophically, this raises the issue of *moral proximity*. Do we owe more to those physically close to us, or those structurally disadvantaged by the same systems we have managed to escape? If a person in Venezuela moves wealth into crypto to avoid hyperinflation, few would call that selfish. If a tech executive in Silicon Valley does the same in order to minimise tax exposure, the moral calculus shifts. Not because the act itself is different, but because its *effects and context* are. *Self-protection is not judged in a vacuum; it is judged in relationship to power, privilege, and opportunity cost.*

This is why ethical asset protection requires more than clever structuring. It requires *intentional transparency*—at least within one's circle of responsibility. The sovereign individual is not just an autonomous actor. They are also a node in a network of trust. To build resilience that does not breed resentment, one must build it in ways that are legible and accessible to others. That may mean sharing tools, teaching strategies, or helping others build parallel paths. What matters is not that protection exists—it's that it doesn't become a moat no one else can cross.

This does not mean one must martyr oneself. The idea that ethical people must suffer in solidarity with those who are less prepared is a corrosive form of moralism. It disincentivises resilience and promotes performative vulnerability. No one is saved by your collapse. You are not a better citizen, parent, or partner because you failed to act prudently. *The real ethical challenge is not whether to protect—it is whether to hoard.*

History is instructive here. From war-torn cities to collapsing economies, those who prepared in advance were not merely the ones who survived—they were often the ones who helped rebuild. But the most respected figures in those scenarios were not the ones who hoarded gold and disappeared. They were the ones who *shared water, rerouted supplies, or used their access to open exits for others.* Protection becomes noble when it is coupled with *responsibility for others.* Without that, it curdles into isolationism. *With it, it becomes leadership.*

This is why preparation must be framed as *service-oriented sovereignty.* You do not build resilience because you fear the world. You build it because the world, as it stands, is unstable—and because you *intend* to help navigate others through that instability. You do not prepare because you want to live above others. You prepare so that you are not *dependent* on systems that may harm both you *and* them. And you do not exit the system because you disdain society. You exit because you want to re-enter on better terms—*terms you help shape.*

So, is protection selfish? Only if it ends with you.

Walking the Line Between Privacy and Paranoia – Balancing Protection and Mental Peace

There is a subtle but growing burden carried by those who value privacy in the 21st century: *a creeping anxiety that the very act of securing one's life can become a source of unrelenting mental noise.* At what point does vigilance become obsession? How much data minimisation is prudent—and how much is pathological? And is it still possible to live with freedom, joy, and clarity while maintaining genuine protection from surveillance, exploitation, or seizure?

This chapter addresses not only the *strategies* of privacy, but the *psychology* of living privately—without descending into paranoia, disconnection, or perpetual fear. Because the truth is this: *paranoia is not protection.* And privacy that comes at the cost of trust, peace of mind, or basic human connection often becomes a hollow victory—more prison than shield.

First, we must recognise the fundamental shift in context. Privacy is no longer a passive default; it is an active choice that requires skill, intention, and often, trade-offs. In the analog world, one had to be targeted in order to be watched. Today, surveillance is ambient, normalised, automated. It is not directed at individuals; it is harvested at scale. Default exposure is the new baseline.

This leads some to adopt radical countermeasures: de-Googling their lives, encrypting every device, rejecting smartphones, using burner SIMs, and shielding their homes from smart appliances. And while these measures may serve specific purposes—particularly for journalists, dissidents, whistleblowers, or others at elevated risk—they often impose a psychological cost disproportionate to their real-world utility. *Security is not simply about what you protect—it's about what it costs you to maintain that protection.*

So how do we draw the line? How do we distinguish necessary safeguards from compulsive overreach?

The answer lies in the principle of *threat modelling*. This is the bedrock of rational privacy strategy. Rather than adopting every defensive technology available, thoughtful individuals must ask: *Who are my realistic adversaries? What are their capabilities? What assets am I protecting? And what is the risk-to-cost ratio of each defence?* This exercise is not only practical—it is calming. It replaces abstract dread with concrete reasoning.

Consider a business owner operating in a volatile jurisdiction. Their risks may include financial surveillance, asset freeze, or politically motivated audits. For such a person, routing funds through stable jurisdictions, securing communications, and avoiding custodial dependencies are not paranoid—they are essential. But that same individual does not need to run their entire home network through six layers of obfuscation or abandon all use of public cloud storage. *Measured privacy is contextual privacy.*

Psychologically, there's another cost that comes from living in defensive mode: it corrodes trust. When everything is seen through the lens of exposure, risk, or betrayal, even human relationships become suspect. This is not a healthy or sustainable way to live. *Privacy that isolates is a failed strategy.* It may preserve data, but it erodes belonging—one of the deepest needs of any person navigating instability.

This is where philosophical and even spiritual insight is helpful. True privacy is not about total invisibility. It is about *selective disclosure*. It is the ability to choose *who* sees *what*, and *when*. It's not about hiding from the world, but about controlling your interface with it. The most resilient people are not those who have vanished—they are those who remain visible *on their own terms. Strategic visibility is the antidote to both overexposure and alienation.*

Take the example of whistleblowers. Some vanish into anonymity; others choose controlled visibility, leveraging encrypted platforms and decentralised publishing while continuing to build influence and networks. The difference is not simply technical—it's psychological. One posture is driven by fear; the other, by clarity.

Likewise, in asset protection, some individuals obsessively hide every trace of ownership, creating Byzantine legal structures that are legally airtight but functionally paralysing. They live with the constant fear of exposure, unable to move capital freely or adapt to new realities. Others adopt layered but legible strategies—trusts, jurisdictions, distributed digital custody—while maintaining enough flexibility to respond, invest, and assist others. Their peace of mind is not compromised by their defences—it is supported by them.

The same logic applies to digital life. It is tempting to withdraw entirely from social platforms, mobile devices, or cloud ecosystems in a bid for purity. But for most people, these tools are *interfaces with the real world.* They are essential to work, relationships, and community. The better approach is to *use them on purpose.* A hardened browser setup, encrypted messaging, non-trackable payments, and compartmentalised identities go further than total abstention. *Privacy is not about disappearance—it is about discretion.*

Historically, we see this distinction in the figures who lived under surveillance states. In East Germany, some citizens lived double lives under the Stasi: public compliance paired with private resistance. Others chose withdrawal—silent, invisible, politically inert. In hindsight, it is often those who found a middle path—*visible enough to shape society, secure enough to survive its collapse*—who left the greatest impact.

From a psychological standpoint, the key is to avoid *hypervigilance.* This is the state of being constantly alert to threats, scanning one's environment for danger, and never truly relaxing. It is common in people who've experienced institutional betrayal, financial seizure, or unjust targeting. But left unchecked, it becomes its own form of trauma—paranoia dressed up as prudence.

To mitigate this, *ritualise your privacy.* Build standard operating procedures that reduce the mental load: weekly key checks, monthly threat audits, clear hierarchies of digital trust. Think like a pilot, not a panicker. The goal is not to live in constant reaction—but to live in *calm readiness.*

Also vital: maintain a sense of *proportionality.* If protecting a particular device requires three hours a day and renders your communications inert, it is not protection—it is paralysis. If safeguarding an account makes it impossible to collaborate, the protection defeats its own purpose. *Resilience is only real if it integrates into real life.*

There's also an ethical layer worth acknowledging. Obsessive privacy can become a form of privilege hoarding. Those with the means to go dark, buy anonymity, or opt out of exposure may inadvertently widen the visibility gap—leaving the less resourced to bear the brunt of the system's gaze. A better approach is to *build and share usable privacy.* Teach others. Fund tools. Strengthen networks. Privacy is more durable when it is *networked*, not hoarded.

In the end, the balance between privacy and paranoia rests on two questions: *Does your protection serve your life—or has it become your life? And does your vigilance increase your peace—or erode it?* There are no fixed thresholds, but there are unmistakable signs. If you can no longer trust anyone, adapt to new contexts, or enjoy your freedoms, then the line has been crossed. The answer is not to abandon privacy, but to *rebalance it*—anchoring it to clarity, connection, and proportionality.

The true goal of privacy is not control. It is dignity. Not fear, but freedom. *And that goal is only achieved when privacy is integrated—not idolised.*

What You Owe, What You Don't – Exploring the Ethics and Strategy of Financial Civil Disobedience

There is a moment—quiet but seismic—when a citizen stops asking "what must I pay?" and begins asking "*what am I truly obligated to support?*" It is not an economic question. It is a moral and philosophical one. And for the financially aware, especially those navigating fragile states, extractive institutions, or accelerating global volatility, it can evolve into something deeper still: *a form of peaceful resistance.* This is the conceptual terrain of financial civil disobedience.

To understand the stakes, we must begin by acknowledging a hard truth: *systems do not always reward the just or the prudent—they often reward the compliant.* And this compliance is not always voluntary. Governments, through taxation, inflation, surveillance, and regulation, have gradually tightened their grip over individual financial sovereignty. In response, an emerging class of global citizens is quietly but deliberately redrawing the boundary between civic duty and institutional consent.

To be clear: financial civil disobedience is not evasion. It is not fraud, deception, or delinquency. *It is intentional noncompliance with financial norms that are deemed illegitimate, unethical, or predatory.* It is Rosa Parks refusing to give up her seat. It is Gandhi's Salt March. It is not about refusing to pay—it is about refusing to *fund.*

In practical terms, this often begins with a simple pivot: *refusing to store wealth in instruments controlled by unreliable actors*. For some, it means exiting fiat currencies vulnerable to hyperinflation or devaluation. For others, it means opting out of mandatory state pension systems in favour of self-directed alternatives. In more advanced expressions, it may involve relocating assets offshore, adopting non-custodial technologies, or minimising taxable presence across jurisdictions. All are acts of control—but not all are acts of rebellion. The distinction lies in intent.

To assess legitimacy, one must evaluate the *morality* of a state's financial demands. In liberal democracies with accountable governance, progressive taxation can be defensible as a mechanism of public goods. But in regimes where taxes fund oppression, corruption, or state violence, moral obligation becomes ambiguous. *Is it ethical to comply with a system that converts your income into weaponised power?* Or does one have a duty to withdraw participation?

This is not a theoretical dilemma. Consider Zimbabwe in the 2000s, where citizens watched the value of their savings vanish overnight under hyperinflation. Or Venezuela, where capital controls and aggressive nationalisations punished basic financial independence. In both cases, those who resisted—by using black-market exchange rates, smuggling goods, or buying crypto assets—were not criminals in any ethical sense. They were *engaged in civil disobedience with a financial form.*

The same logic appears in subtler contexts. When a government bails out corporations that harm the environment, surveils citizens en masse, or penalises small entrepreneurs through punitive regulation, compliance ceases to be a neutral act. *Funding dysfunction is itself a contribution to dysfunction.* This realisation is the root of the quiet rebellion now spreading among digital nomads, decentralised workers, and capital allocators seeking not just return—but integrity.

Critics may argue that opting out is selfish—that those who can afford to escape bear a duty to stay and reform the system from within. But this critique rests on a dangerous assumption: that reform is always possible from within. History suggests otherwise. In states where dissent is criminalised, elections are manipulated, and courts are co-opted, reform becomes performance—symbolic rather than structural.

Financial exit, by contrast, is *nonviolent leverage*. It shifts power by withholding capital. It forces regimes to compete for legitimacy. This is the silent genius of jurisdictional arbitrage: *governments now operate in a global marketplace of credibility*. If a state becomes predatory, it loses not just moral authority—but *capital*, talent, and investment. In this way, civil disobedience becomes civil negotiation.

But there is nuance. Not all noncompliance is ethical. There is a world of difference between the billionaire hiding wealth in shell companies to dodge civic responsibility, and the middle-class saver shielding assets from a kleptocratic regime. *Civil disobedience must always be rooted in discernment, not convenience.* The question is not simply "how do I pay less?" but "*what structures deserve my trust, and which no longer do?*"

There is also a psychological toll. Practising financial disobedience often requires *decoupling from institutional identity*. The obedient citizen becomes the conscious dissident. This shift can feel isolating, especially in cultures that valorise obedience or demonise dissent. It takes intellectual courage to admit: *I do not owe the system everything it demands.*

Yet it is this precise discernment that defines the mature sovereign individual. *Freedom is not given; it is managed.* And managing freedom often means establishing ethical boundaries around one's participation. What do I owe to the common good? What do I owe to future generations? What do I owe to a regime that refuses to reciprocate respect?

There are no universal answers—but there are recurring principles. You owe participation where your contribution creates mutual benefit. You do not owe participation where your contribution enables harm. You owe transparency to those who have earned your trust. You do not owe visibility to institutions that weaponise it. You owe taxes that build. You do not owe tribute that destroys.

Practically speaking, this mindset is expressed not just in tax decisions, but in portfolio strategy. Consider the individual who reduces exposure to central bank currencies by allocating into decentralised stablecoins, gold, or real estate held in protective trusts. Or the entrepreneur who launches in Estonia via e-residency, minimising friction and maximising sovereignty. Or the family who moves their educational fund out of a faltering national bank into a Swiss or Singaporean custodian, prioritising continuity over loyalty. These are not illegal acts. They are *deliberate acts of boundary-setting.*

Civil disobedience also extends into consumption. Choosing not to fund exploitative megacorps, surveillance platforms, or rent-seeking intermediaries is part of a broader financial ethic. So is peer-to-peer commerce, decentralised contracting, and community-level investment. Each act is a vote—a redirection of value from hierarchy to agency.

And yet, restraint is vital. *Civil disobedience should never become financial nihilism.* The goal is not to sever all ties or romanticise anarchy. The goal is to *reshape the moral architecture of value flow.* It is about standing inside the system, with one hand on the lever and the other on the plug.

Ultimately, financial civil disobedience is a form of moral accounting. It asks not just how wealth is earned or spent, but *how it is aligned with conscience.* It is the decision to live not merely within legality—but within integrity.

The path is neither easy nor clean. It may bring scrutiny, friction, or sacrifice. But it also brings clarity. It forces the essential question: *Do I fund the future I believe in—or the one I merely survive?*

That question will define the next generation of financially conscious citizens—not as consumers of systems, but as curators of them.

Becoming a Steward, Not a Hoarder – Reframing Asset Protection as a Duty to Self and Future Generations

It is not difficult to hide. With sufficient resources, an individual can sequester capital behind encrypted ledgers, arcane trusts, or sovereign jurisdictions. What is far more difficult—and far more urgent—is learning how to *hold* with intention. In times of uncertainty, when systems fracture and trust in institutions decays, asset protection is often mistaken for a defensive act. But the act of *preserving value* is not the end of the story. It is the beginning of a different responsibility: stewardship.

To become a steward is to understand that wealth—however earned, inherited, or accumulated—is not static capital to be buried in digital vaults, but *stored energy* that must be directed with care. It requires an ethical shift away from scarcity thinking and towards *intergenerational foresight.* That shift, however, is deeply countercultural.

The prevailing economic narrative rewards accumulation. Society treats wealth as a scorecard, a fortress, a moat. Much of modern finance, both retail and institutional, operates on the premise that more is inherently better, that protection means insulation, and that financial success is measured by what one can keep from others. But hoarding is not strategy. *It is paralysis dressed as prudence.*

Consider the pathology of over-conservation: families that bury assets in illiquid trusts they barely understand, investors who stack gold without an endgame, entrepreneurs who refuse to deploy capital for fear of taxation or loss. These behaviours mimic prudence, but they undermine resilience. *Protection without purpose becomes self-sabotage.*

Stewardship demands more. It asks, first and foremost: *What is this capital for?* And further: *Who, besides me, must benefit from its security?*

For those building sovereign portfolios, these are not sentimental questions—they are strategic imperatives. A sovereign asset base is not simply a shelter from inflation, seizure, or collapse. It is a mechanism for continuity. And continuity is not measured by what survives a crisis, but by *what emerges useful afterward.*

Let's interrogate the difference. A hoarder prepares for a world that doesn't change. A steward prepares *so that value can adapt to what comes next.* A hoarder sees others as threats. A steward recognises others as *stakeholders*. A hoarder optimises for control. A steward optimises for *coherence*—financial, ethical, generational.

This reframing has practical consequences. For instance, asset diversification under a stewardship model no longer ends at geographic hedging or asset-class distribution. It includes *time horizons of meaning*. That is: What assets can I deploy today to protect my autonomy? What structures must I build to ensure my children's freedom? What institutions do I fund—or refuse to fund—based on their alignment with long-term values?

In this context, even the choice of storage becomes political. Custodial banking in fragile jurisdictions is not just risky—it's negligent. Similarly, over-allocation to opaque hedge funds or speculative tokens without discernible social utility may reflect not strategic foresight, but *an addiction to opacity*. Stewardship begins where transparency meets intention.

It's worth looking at families that have succeeded across generations—not in scale of wealth, but in continuity of influence. The Rothschilds, the Rockefellers, the Agnelli dynasty: these are not merely stories of inheritance, but of *institutional stewardship*. They built frameworks—trusts, endowments, philanthropic funds—not just to avoid taxes, but to *codify values*. And those values shaped the capital. They directed it across time.

But you need not be born into wealth to adopt this approach. The modern steward uses decentralised tools, legal structures, and geographic arbitrage *not merely to protect value, but to channel it with meaning*. A self-custodied wallet is not just a place to store Bitcoin—it is a commitment to *sovereign infrastructure*. A properly structured private foundation is not just a tax-advantaged wrapper—it is a vehicle for legacy. A diversified citizenship portfolio is not just an insurance policy—it is an articulation of where you *believe freedom can still thrive*.

Contrast this with the corrosive instincts of hoarding. When wealth is held only to soothe anxiety, it metastasises into fear. It generates defensive action. It encourages asset stagnation, over-risk aversion, and isolation. It silences philanthropy. It distorts time preference. Most dangerously, it *disconnects capital from consequence.*

That disconnection is everywhere. High-net-worth individuals who store fortunes in offshore accounts they will never use. Mid-tier investors so obsessed with market volatility that they lose sight of strategic opportunity. Even decentralised finance participants who build layer upon layer of security—but never deploy for productive use. These are not acts of courage. They are rituals of containment.

To move beyond them, one must confront a simple truth: *Wealth is most powerful when it moves intelligently.* That doesn't mean reckless spending. It means *directed deployment,* guided by principles that outlast panic. For the steward, this could look like allocating part of one's crypto holdings to privacy-enhancing infrastructure. Or seeding regenerative agriculture in politically neutral zones. Or designing multi-jurisdictional trusts that insulate heirs from authoritarian interference while preserving alignment with core values. These are not acts of resistance alone—they are acts of *design.*

Design, in this context, implies responsibility. It demands *knowledge of the tools* (legal, financial, technological), but also *discernment of the moment.* What threats are rising? What systems are eroding? What opportunities remain uncaptured because the capital to pursue them is locked in fear-based structures?

The rise of the sovereign individual does not absolve one from duty—it *amplifies it.* With greater control comes greater responsibility for how wealth is protected, used, and eventually transferred. The steward understands that the point of security is not to hoard in the dark, but to *preserve agency in the light*—for self, for family, for networks of trust that may one day carry the torch forward.

Psychologically, this requires evolving past survivalism. It demands a mindset that views resilience not as insulation, but as *capacity for useful action under pressure*. That capacity is deeply compromised when capital is treated as sacred rather than strategic. Just as liquidity must be accessible, so too must our principles about why we store, what we store, and whom we store it for.

And yet, stewardship is not martyrdom. It is not about giving everything away or rejecting caution. It is about *constructive calibration*: protecting wealth so that it remains functional across collapse scenarios, but also *investable in times of rebuilding*. The true steward sees beyond the bunker.

The next decade will not reward passivity. As inflation bites, institutions fragment, and new jurisdictions rise, asset protection will no longer be an option—it will be a precondition for autonomy. But those who frame protection solely as a means of exclusion—who build only walls—will find themselves encased in their own irrelevance. The world will move. So must capital. So must the mind that governs it.

To become a steward is to reject the false binary between protection and contribution. It is to say: *I will protect not because I fear the world, but because I intend to engage with it—deliberately, intelligently, and intergenerationally*. That is not hoarding. That is strategy infused with duty.

Chapter 10
Exercises in Sovereignty

Sovereignty isn't an abstraction. It's not a theory to be admired from afar. It is, at its core, a skill—acquired, sharpened, and exercised.

In the chapters leading up to this one, we've mapped the frameworks and philosophies that support wealth preservation in unstable times. We've discussed structure, context, and the shifting foundations upon which value is built. But ideas, however rigorous, don't keep you free when systems begin to fail. The time has come to cross that line—from contemplation to execution. From understanding volatility to moving through it with practiced, deliberate steps.

Think of this chapter as your proving ground. *Exercises in Sovereignty* is where principle meets protocol, where intellectual clarity is translated into operational muscle. It's not about what to believe—it's about what to *do* when belief alone is no longer enough.

This pivot matters deeply. Because wealth, in times of disruption, is not simply what you have. It's what you can *reach*—what you can activate, redirect, protect. Knowing the theoretical vulnerabilities of banking systems or the limitations of fiat is of limited use if you can't respond fluidly when they crack. And they *will* crack, often without warning. Precision—not panic—is the discipline required here. This is your tactical manual, your field guide to real-world sovereignty.

At the centre of that preparedness is a truth you won't often hear from the wealth management industry: asset protection is inherently contextual. What holds firm in one crisis may unravel in another. A buffer against inflation could become a trap under capital controls. A liquidity solution in peacetime might morph into a liability under political targeting. Sovereignty, then, must be modular—layered, mobile, responsive to the specific contours of emerging threat environments. Not rigid doctrine, but a living system.

This is why we begin with the Three-Scenario Exit Plan. No, it's not a tinfoil-hat exercise in paranoia. It's the modern equivalent of a business continuity strategy—but crafted for personal autonomy rather than shareholder value. The plan centres on three destabilising forces: currency devaluation, banking system failure, and targeted political pressure. Each scenario requires a distinct choreography of asset movement, jurisdictional positioning, and mental readiness. The real question it forces is stark but essential: if your world fractured tomorrow, what could you access—and how quickly?

From this foundation, we move into the Sovereignty Scorecard. This is not a toy or a branding gimmick. It's a mirror—an unflinching inventory of your operational strength and exposure. In a culture saturated with performative sovereignty (the buzzwords, the bravado, the "trustless" evangelism), the Scorecard clears the fog. Can you, in practice, migrate your digital assets without external gatekeepers? Do you hold passports from more than one political regime? Are your income flows decoupled from single-point-of-failure institutions? Can you mobilise liquidity across borders when banks become bottlenecks? These aren't abstractions. They're litmus tests. And they expose the gap between intention and implementation.

But diagnosis alone isn't enough. Which is why the chapter culminates in Your Silent Vault Blueprint—a strategy not just for preserving wealth, but for doing so *discreetly, defensively, and decisively.* This isn't legacy estate planning. It's not designed for probate courts and tax efficiency brochures. It's crafted for the real world, the sharp-edge world. A world where the knock on the door doesn't always come with a warrant, and where asset safety must be rehearsed, not hoped for. Your Silent Vault spans domains—digital custody, physical access, legal insulation, geographic diversification, psychological resilience. It's not about retreat. It's about knowing—unambiguously—what you hold, where it lives, and how to move it, fast and frictionless, without having to raise your hand for permission.

To be very clear: this isn't a manifesto for the frightened. It's a manual for the prepared. Sovereignty in this sense isn't a bunker. It's agility. The ability to exit hostile environments, reroute capital with stealth, and maintain both continuity and control when systems around you buckle. The sovereign operator is not a doomsday fantasist—they are a strategist who sees further, plans wider, and prepares deeper than the headlines allow.

And if you're still here—reading, absorbing, interrogating—you're not here for ideology. You're here for competence. That means letting go of glossy institutional promises, the false comfort of "too big to fail," and the unearned confidence in platforms that can be shut down with a flick of bureaucratic will. It means learning the slow, sometimes tedious, but always critical disciplines of self-custody, multi-jurisdictional architecture, legal shielding, income autonomy. In short, you're here to build resilience that isn't borrowed.

This chapter won't flatter you. It asks you to confront your soft spots, the assumptions you've never stress-tested, the places you've allowed faith to replace systems. It pushes you to simulate breakdown—not because collapse is certain, but because *uncertainty* is. And what you earn for doing that work is not fear—but readiness. Conviction that's been tested.

Let's be honest: this isn't about fleeing. It's about being able to *move*—on your own terms, with your eyes open, and your hands steady. Whether it's inflation biting overnight, a sudden freeze on withdrawals, or the quiet tightening of a compliance noose, you should not be scrambling. You should be executing.

What you're building now isn't a set of bullet points. It's an operating system. Responsive. Durable. Evolutionary. And when the moment comes—as it inevitably does—where most people are stuck blinking at the screen, paralysed by events, you'll already be in motion. Quietly. Deliberately. Ahead of the curve.

That, in the end, is the line that separates awareness from preparedness. Theory from capacity. Possession from sovereignty.

And with that—let's begin.

The Hidden Wealth Audit – Reviewing Holdings Through a Vulnerability Lens

Most people know what they own, but few understand what they *expose*. This is the first uncomfortable truth a true asset protection strategy must confront. Wealth, despite its surface visibility in balance sheets and brokerage statements, often hides its own fragility. What appears diversified may be clustered. What looks liquid may be gated. What feels private may be trivially surveilled. What seems yours may—in legal, jurisdictional, or technical terms—belong to someone else the moment trust is tested. To confront this requires more than a spreadsheet. It demands a *vulnerability lens.*

A Hidden Wealth Audit is not an accounting exercise. It is a diagnostic inquiry designed to surface one thing: *where your sovereignty is most at risk*. It asks what percentage of your holdings are custodial, jurisdiction-bound, surveillance-prone, easily frozen, difficult to transfer, or exposed to inflation, taxation, litigation, or political interference. The goal is not merely to quantify assets but to *qualify their resilience.* And that requires a shift in thinking—from portfolio performance to existential accessibility.

This chapter is not about building wealth. It is about stress-testing it.

Why Traditional Audits Conceal More Than They Reveal

Traditional audits are retrospective. They evaluate efficiency, returns, and tax alignment. But they are blind to structural vulnerabilities. A high-performing asset is not necessarily a secure one. For example, an index fund held in a major U.S. brokerage account may be growing steadily on paper—until access is throttled during a platform outage, a political freeze, or a contested residency status. A real estate portfolio may appreciate impressively—while being jurisdictionally captive, illiquid under duress, and exposed to confiscatory property taxes.

This is not alarmism. It is *functional realism*. History offers countless moments when asset control was revoked or restricted without warning. Argentine bank account seizures (2001), Cypriot bail-ins (2013), India's cash demonetisation (2016), Canadian financial account freezes during protests (2022)—each of these events punished assumptions of permanence and access. The assets themselves were not flawed. But the *context* shifted—and the holders lacked the means to pivot.

A Hidden Wealth Audit rejects the myth of neutral infrastructure. It recognises that every asset exists *within a system*—and systems can change their rules faster than individuals can respond.

Reframing the Definition of 'Safe'

Ask a conventional wealth advisor what constitutes a safe asset and they will default to volatility charts, default risk ratings, and institutional endorsements. But such measures are silent on *confiscation risk*, *mobility latency*, *jurisdictional entanglement*, or *digital censorship*. This is not to dismiss traditional metrics, but to highlight their blind spots. What's needed is a broader taxonomy of vulnerability.

Assets must now be assessed across a different axis:

Custodial exposure: Who actually holds your assets? Can access be denied?

Jurisdictional concentration: Are your holdings tied to a single legal system?

Portability under pressure: How quickly can value be moved or reallocated?

Censorship resistance: Can use or transfer be restricted based on political, social, or personal identity criteria?

Legal insulation: Are your assets shielded from arbitrary seizure, litigation, or expropriation?

Currency dependency: Are your holdings tied to the fate of a single inflation-prone unit of account?

These categories may not appear on your bank statement—but they determine whether you *control your assets in practice*, or merely on paper.

From Inventory to Insight: Conducting the Audit

The Hidden Wealth Audit begins with a full-spectrum inventory—not just of what you own, but *how* you own it. At first glance, this might resemble a traditional asset map. But instead of asking "how much is it worth?" we ask: *How exposed is it?*

Consider a simplified example:

A person holds:

£300,000 in real estate (primary home)

£150,000 in a brokerage index fund (UK-based custodian)

£50,000 in a pension (government-regulated scheme)

£20,000 in cryptocurrency (held on a centralised exchange)

£5,000 in cash (bank account)

£3,000 in precious metals (kept at home)

On paper, this is a net worth of £528,000. But when assessed through a vulnerability lens, cracks appear:

The primary home is non-portable, jurisdiction-bound, and subject to property tax or forced sale.

The brokerage fund and pension are custodial and potentially subject to political interference or capital controls.

Cryptocurrency on a centralised exchange is vulnerable to platform risk and custodial freezing.

The bank-held cash is at risk of inflation, surveillance, and withdrawal restrictions.

Only the small stash of physical metals escapes digital or jurisdictional dependencies.

From a sovereignty standpoint, more than 90% of this wealth is either *non-portable*, *custodial*, or *system-exposed.* The true "freedom-weighted" net worth might be less than £20,000—once conditions turn hostile.

This insight is not intended to provoke fear. It is meant to *awaken clarity*. It enables forward strategy—not reactionary scrambling.

The Psychology of Hidden Exposure

A wealth audit conducted through a vulnerability lens will often reveal more *emotional risk* than financial risk. Many individuals—even those who intellectually grasp sovereign finance—harbour an unconscious belief in institutional continuity. They imagine "my country would never", "my broker is too big to fail", "I'll move it when things get worse." This cognitive bias—status quo anchoring—creates paralysis.

The Hidden Wealth Audit forces these assumptions to the surface. It confronts the psyche with this question: *What if the conditions you rely on disappear faster than you can adapt?*

This is not a theoretical concern. In 2022, Russian nationals with assets in Western banks and brokerages learned overnight that their citizenship—not any criminal act—was grounds for access denial. In Turkey and Argentina, currency collapse did not announce itself—it accelerated past prediction. In Lebanon, bank deposits vanished into enforced withdrawal limits with no legal recourse.

Such moments reveal the cost of *delay*. The audit, then, is not only a financial map—it is a psychological mirror. It shows where you are telling yourself stories to avoid hard decisions.

Ethical and Strategic Reflections

Does a Hidden Wealth Audit encourage hoarding? No. It encourages *resilient stewardship*. By understanding the practical limits of each asset class and jurisdictional link, individuals can make wiser decisions—not to hide wealth, but to *preserve its functionality*.

Some will ask: "Isn't this overly defensive? Shouldn't we trust legal systems to uphold property rights?" Ideally, yes. But *strategy is not about ideals—it's about contingencies*. Responsible wealth holders don't abandon systems—they prepare for their failure without fanfare.

And there's an ethical dimension too. Sovereign wealth management enables *continuity of support*. Those who can preserve access to value are often better positioned to help others when systems fail. The audit, then, becomes an act of foresight—not selfishness. *You cannot stabilise others if you are destabilised yourself.*

From Insight to Action

The audit is the beginning—not the end. Once vulnerabilities are revealed, the next step is reallocation: balancing liquid, semi-liquid, and immovable assets across multiple vectors of jurisdiction, custody, and access. This includes:

Transitioning from custodial to self-custodied crypto holdings

Rebalancing property exposure with portable stores of value

Establishing legal structures to shield against litigation or overreach

Diversifying income streams across borders and platforms

Relocating partial capital to favourable jurisdictions

These shifts are not wholesale abandonment of traditional finance. They are strategic decentralisations. They restore optionality—without announcing it.

Final Thought: Auditing in a Shifting World

In a world where rules can shift faster than you can react, *clarity becomes currency*. The Hidden Wealth Audit is not a one-time exercise. It is a recurring ritual. Every quarter, every fiscal year, every major legislative shift—return to the audit. Ask again: *What do I truly control? What is vulnerable? What must be redesigned?*

The sovereign individual is not one who owns the most—but one who is least exposed when assumptions break. And exposure is not just a risk. *It's a choice—until it isn't.*

Now is the time to choose.

Your Three-Scenario Exit Plan – Preparing for Inflation, Bank Seizure, and Political Crisis

Wealth, security, and mobility are never tested under normal conditions. They are tested in the moment the system around you begins to buckle—when capital is frozen, currencies are debased, or a previously stable government turns inward, punitive, or chaotic. At that point, what matters is not how much you have, but *how fast you can move*, *what you can still access*, and *which rules still protect you*. A Three-Scenario Exit Plan is not a fringe precaution. It is the *bare minimum* of financial maturity in a world where systemic volatility is no longer an abstract geopolitical risk, but a recurring feature of the global order.

Let's be clear: the point of planning for collapse is *not* to predict it. It is to prevent being paralysed by it. Catastrophe rarely respects ideologies. Argentina did not ask whether you were pro-regulation before freezing accounts in 2001. Cyprus did not inquire about your long-term trust in banking before executing a 47.5% bail-in in 2013. And no government asked whether you agreed with their policies before imposing capital controls, lockdowns, or protests bans. The time to design optionality is *before* you need it.

This chapter offers a rigorous framework for preparing specifically for three high-likelihood disruption scenarios: monetary debasement (inflation), institutional failure (bank seizure), and political repression (crisis or authoritarian shift). Each scenario is structurally distinct, yet strategically connected. And each requires a sober, specific, and quietly executable exit plan that turns panic into preemption.

Scenario 1: Inflation – When the Currency Ceases to Keep Its Promise

Inflation, when it accelerates, is not simply a monetary failure. It is a betrayal of the very contract upon which civil economic life is based—that value stored today will not evaporate tomorrow. This is not theoretical. Lebanon, Venezuela, Zimbabwe, Argentina, and even Turkey and Nigeria have lived through currency collapses in the last two decades. And even in so-called "developed" economies, real inflation has exceeded reported inflation consistently, punishing savers and wage earners while rewarding the leveraged and well-advised.

The first exit plan is not geographic—it is *monetary*. It asks: *What happens if the currency in which you're denominated becomes structurally unreliable?*

Your response must be multi-layered:

Store value outside fiat: This includes hard assets like gold and silver, decentralised assets like Bitcoin (not ETFs—self-custodied), and even productive equity denominated in more stable jurisdictions.

Benchmark your wealth in purchasing power, not digits: Do not be seduced by nominal portfolio growth. If your grocery basket costs 20% more but your account shows a 10% increase, you are poorer.

Maintain an inflation counterbalance: Real estate in stable jurisdictions, ownership of cash-flowing businesses with price-adjustment mechanisms, and minimal local cash exposure are critical.

An inflation exit plan is not about fleeing your country. It's about *hedging your operating system*. The critical insight: *Currency is not wealth. It is a temporary interface with the market. Don't confuse it for the thing it represents.*

Scenario 2: Bank Seizure – When Access Is Denied Without Warning

A bank seizure is not always called a "seizure". Sometimes it's a freeze. Sometimes a "holiday". Sometimes it is a withdrawal limit justified by liquidity crises. Other times it takes the form of judicial garnishments, tax liens, or regulatory suspicion. Regardless of form, the function is the same: your assets become theirs. Temporarily or permanently. The question is: *Can you operate when your institutionally held capital vanishes behind a policy decision or a server error?*

A viable bank-seizure exit plan includes:

At least one non-custodial reserve: If your entire liquidity profile is dependent on institutional goodwill (banks, brokers, payment platforms), you do not own liquidity—you rent it.

Diversified custody jurisdictions: Multiple bank accounts in multiple countries may seem excessive—until one system locks you out. Cross-border liquidity is a pressure valve, not a luxury.

Cash-equivalent independence: Self-custodied digital assets, precious metals, or even physical foreign currency in secured locations provide short-term continuity in the event of systemic lockout.

Case in point: In 2022, ordinary Russians—uninvolved in their government's politics—lost access to international banking in under 48 hours. In Canada, peaceful protest participants had their accounts frozen under emergency laws. A seizure scenario does not require illegality on your part. It requires *only one government's decision* to draw the line, and your assets being in the wrong place.

The strategic imperative: *Do not centralise access. Resilience is redundancy.*

Scenario 3: Political Crisis – When Your Freedom Becomes a Liability

What if the problem is not economic, but civic? What if the institutions themselves turn hostile—not through incompetence, but intent? In times of political instability, dissenters become targets, minorities become scapegoats, and previous legal protections can be suspended in the name of national interest or public safety.

This scenario does not always begin with martial law. Sometimes it begins with surveillance, regulatory overreach, or the weaponisation of tax codes. What matters is not how it begins—but whether you're exposed *without recourse.*

Your political crisis exit plan must address three domains:

Physical relocation: You cannot negotiate with a failed state from within its borders. Second residency or citizenship, safehouse access, and visa-free mobility are not fringe issues—they are survival infrastructure.

Data decentralisation: Political shifts often bring censorship, internet controls, or digital ID mandates. Your critical records, financial access, and communication platforms must be sovereign and encrypted.

Community coordination: In a crisis, your network matters more than your bank account. Encrypted trust-based groups, diaspora alliances, and support nodes (local and international) form your real defence grid.

It is not enough to say "it won't happen here". That assumption has failed in Myanmar, Hong Kong, Ethiopia, Sri Lanka, Ukraine, and beyond—all in just the last decade. The logic of liberty is this: *You cannot wait until it is endangered to build your off-switch.*

Designing the Actual Plan – Quiet, Modular, Executable

An exit plan is useless if it lives only in theory. Each of these three scenarios demands practical translation. At the very minimum, this includes:

A clearly documented private asset map (offline, encrypted backup)

A list of go-to jurisdictions for rapid capital redeployment

Access to mobile capital reserves (crypto, metals, foreign cash)

Second passport or long-term visa/residency options in progress

Emergency comms and coordination protocols with family or trusted peers

More sophisticated versions include offshore legal entities, multi-country banking, dual-citizen tax preparation, decentralised income streams, and silent vault blueprints. But even a partial plan is vastly superior to none. The objective is *minimum fragility*. Not immortality.

It's also critical to *practise execution.* That may mean:

Testing the withdrawal of large bank amounts and noting delays

Transferring crypto assets between cold wallets

Researching embassy timelines for secondary passport countries

Conducting simulation scenarios with your family or business partners

Planning is not paranoia. *It is peace of mind earned in advance.*

Ethical Framing: Is Planning for Collapse Selfish or Strategic?

Some readers will ask: is it selfish to prepare for systemic failure while others remain exposed? But the opposite may be true. The sovereign individual, properly resourced and ethically anchored, becomes *a stabilising force.* The person with access to capital, legal tools, and safe zones can assist others, protect dependents, and maintain principled action when institutions cannot.

The Three-Scenario Exit Plan is not an escape from society. It is the scaffolding required to remain functional within it—*even when it fails to meet its side of the contract.*

Final Insight: Exit Is Not Always Physical—But It Must Be Possible

The most dangerous condition for any individual is to be *trapped.* Not just physically, but financially, legally, and digitally. What these three scenarios demand is the ability to exit a failing system—*on your own terms.* Not always by leaving it, but by *transcending its control.* That may mean moving money, moving information, or moving yourself. But the point is: *you must be the one who decides.*

Systems are increasingly complex, centralised, and fragile. Resilience is not passive. It is designed.

The Three-Scenario Exit Plan is your blueprint.

Make it while the lights are still on.

Sovereignty Scorecard – Measuring the Truth About Your Financial Control

Most people believe they own their wealth. In reality, they lease it—often without reading the fine print. The appearance of control is not control. A number on a screen is not the same as access. A signed title deed is not the same as unencumbered use. And a password-protected account is not the same as irrevocable ownership.

If that sounds alarmist, it is only because so many have normalised fragility. When wealth depends on permissions, intermediaries, and jurisdictional assumptions, what we call "ownership" is often contingent. Sovereignty, by contrast, means something very different. It means *functional, provable, and portable control* over your assets—regardless of systemic stress, policy shifts, or institutional failure.

The Sovereignty Scorecard is not a gimmick. It is an analytical tool designed to *quantify* your financial autonomy. It surfaces what most asset statements obscure: *how easily can your wealth be frozen, taxed without recourse, diluted, confiscated, mispriced, or denied under emergency logic?*

Unlike a net worth sheet, which answers "How much?", the Sovereignty Scorecard answers "*How free?*".

Why Measurement Matters: Because Illusions Are Expensive

Control over one's wealth is not binary—it is a spectrum. The same amount of capital held in two different forms can represent radically different levels of freedom. A £100,000 bond portfolio in a domestic brokerage account is not the same as £100,000 held in a cold-stored decentralised asset. The former can be frozen with a single email from a regulator; the latter requires your private key.

Yet most people measure wealth using conventional metrics: liquidity, yield, volatility, market correlation. These are useful—but partial. They ignore *the governance layer* of wealth: *who can say no to you, and under what pretext?*

The Sovereignty Scorecard introduces that missing axis. It does not replace traditional financial metrics. It complements them with *structural analysis*. And it begins with a very simple premise: *the more conditions attached to your wealth, the less you truly own it.*

The Core Dimensions of Financial Sovereignty

To understand and improve your score, you must dissect wealth across five dimensions. These are not philosophical—they are *functional.* Each dimension can be measured independently, but they are synergistic in practice.

1. **Custody** – Who holds the keys? If you cannot access your assets without third-party approval (a bank, an exchange, a government registry), you do not have sovereignty. Self-custody—when executed securely—is the gold standard.

2. **Jurisdictional Redundancy** – Are your assets exposed to a single legal regime? Sovereignty requires *escape velocity* from any one government's arbitrary reach. This means banking, residencies, trusts, or storage that cross legal and geographic lines.

3. **Access Resilience** – Can you reach your wealth during a system failure? Consider internet outages, currency controls, travel bans, platform deplatforming, or legal overreach. Sovereign wealth must remain *functionally accessible* even in degraded conditions.

4. **Mobility** – Can your capital move without triggering delays, audits, or exit taxes? Portability is crucial in a crisis. An asset you can't liquidate or transfer without alerting the system is not truly yours—it's a hostage.

5. **Conversion Flexibility** – Can your asset be converted into a means of exchange, trade, or security quickly? Gold is sovereign, but not liquid in crisis. Real estate is concrete, but immobile. Balance matters.

These dimensions are not academic. They affect *how and when* you can deploy capital in a moment of need. The Sovereignty Scorecard, therefore, turns the abstract notion of "preparedness" into a *quantifiable profile*—one that can be updated and improved over time.

Case Study: Identical Wealth, Unequal Control

Consider two individuals, both with £500,000 in assets.

Person A has:

£250,000 in a domestic brokerage

£100,000 in a pension fund

£100,000 in a local savings account

£50,000 in equity of a local business

Person B has:

£100,000 in self-custodied Bitcoin

£100,000 in a multi-jurisdictional trust

£100,000 in foreign real estate

£100,000 in cash equivalents across three countries

£100,000 in an income-generating offshore LLC

Both have identical net worths, but Person B has *orders of magnitude more sovereignty*. In the event of a banking crisis, tax seizure, or political clampdown, Person A is trapped. Person B is fluid. Wealth parity means little if one's capital is immobilised when it matters most.

Scoring Yourself Honestly

A real Sovereignty Scorecard assigns weighted scores to each asset across the five dimensions. While there's no universal formula, a credible framework might assign a score between 0 (fragile) and 10 (sovereign) on each metric for each asset. For example:

A self-custodied crypto asset might score:

Custody: 10

Jurisdictional Redundancy: 9

Access Resilience: 9

Mobility: 10

Conversion Flexibility: 7

A pension fund might score:

Custody: 1

Jurisdictional Redundancy: 2

Access Resilience: 2

Mobility: 0

Conversion Flexibility: 1

The result is not just a number, but a profile—a visual and cognitive map of *where you are exposed.* This allows strategic allocation not just by risk tolerance, but by *sovereignty tolerance.* That is a far more meaningful metric for those serious about lasting financial agency.

Beyond Assets: Behavioural and Legal Sovereignty

True financial sovereignty is not just about the architecture of your holdings. It's about *how you behave* and *what legal posture you inhabit.*

Do you default to compliance with every new law, even when it contradicts constitutional precedent or natural justice? Do you rely entirely on a single tax advisor or legal firm? Have you built muscle memory for moving assets quickly, or are your defences entirely theoretical?

Likewise, the legal wrapper matters. Trusts, foundations, offshore entities, and multi-residency strategies are *force multipliers* for sovereignty—if understood and deployed correctly. But blind trust in paperwork is just another form of fragility. Always test the edges.

Behavioural sovereignty also includes the ability to say no—to decline investments, services, or platforms that compromise your principles or privacy in exchange for convenience. A sovereign wealth structure is also a *sovereign mindset.*

Strategic Applications: Why This Matters Now

The world is converging toward centralisation. From central bank digital currencies (CBDCs) to universal ID mandates, from Know-Your-Customer rules to asset reporting networks, *the assumption is that all wealth should be visible, controllable, and taxable at will.* In that context, the Sovereignty Scorecard is not a theoretical tool. It is a form of *counter-mapping*—a way to see your position within the net before it closes.

In nations with capital controls, high inflation, or authoritarian drift, the relevance of sovereignty metrics becomes acute. But even in so-called "safe" democracies, the fragility is rising: pensions are being raided, property rights eroded by regulation, and private capital subordinated to state goals under ESG or AML pretexts.

Ask yourself: *If tomorrow, your accounts were frozen under suspicion—could you function? If the currency was devalued—could you preserve value? If relocation were needed—could you fund it within 24 hours?*

If not, your score is too low. The good news is: *it can be raised.* Quietly. Legally. Proactively.

From Concept to Habit: Making the Scorecard Actionable

To truly benefit from this framework, the Sovereignty Scorecard must become a regular part of your financial review—updated quarterly or semi-annually like any serious audit. Integrate it into your net worth statements. Use it to rebalance. Apply it before any major acquisition or restructure.

And use it to educate those closest to you. Sovereignty is fractal—it weakens if only one member of a family or enterprise understands it. Build the capacity collectively.

Ultimately, the Sovereignty Scorecard is not about fear. It's about *discipline.* The discipline to measure what matters. To face the uncomfortable asymmetries hidden behind portfolio balances. And to transform abstract principles into practical control.

The Final Word: Own Your Wealth, or Be Owned Through It

Financial sovereignty is not a slogan. It is a measurable condition. The Sovereignty Scorecard offers a mirror: not just of what you possess, but *how freely you possess it.* It exposes the gap between apparent wealth and functional agency.

In a world where institutions are becoming more brittle, intrusive, and unpredictable, the ultimate question is not, "How much do you have?" It is, "*What can you still do when they say no?*"

Score honestly. Rebuild methodically. And never confuse compliance with security.

True wealth is not just owned. It is *unbound.*

Your Silent Vault Blueprint – Designing for Quiet Strength in a Noisy World

Asset protection is no longer a matter of wealth preservation alone—it is an expression of strategic autonomy. In a world where financial institutions are increasingly politicised, privacy is treated as suspicion, and access to capital is filtered through layers of compliance, having wealth is not the same as being able to use it freely. Control, not accumulation, has become the essential metric of financial preparedness.

That is why a Silent Vault is not a metaphor. It is a design. A silent vault is a private, durable, modular system for *protecting, accessing, and adapting your capital*—quietly, legally, and under your command. It is silent in that it avoids signalling, dependency, and exposure. And it is a vault not because it sits idle, but because it prioritises *resilience over display, substance over optics.*

This chapter will not hand you a one-size-fits-all formula. It offers something more powerful: a framework for building your own. The Silent Vault Blueprint is a living strategy, tailored to your risk profile, jurisdictional exposures, moral tolerances, and future vision. It is asset protection done with intent, not impulse. With foresight, not fear.

Let us begin by challenging the most dangerous assumption in modern finance: that protection is passive. It is not. It is *architectural.*

Why You Need a Blueprint, Not a Checklist

Too many asset protection efforts fail because they start with tools, not outcomes. People install trust structures, open foreign accounts, or convert savings into hard assets without first articulating *what they are actually protecting against* and *what they require their capital to do under duress.*

The Silent Vault Blueprint reverses that mistake. It begins with the understanding that *every asset choice encodes a prediction about the future.* Holding cash predicts liquidity will be available. Holding property assumes legal stability. Holding equities trusts in market integrity. All can be rational—but none are riskless.

The blueprint therefore starts by *mapping assumptions.* These must be surfaced and interrogated honestly:

What scenarios am I defending against: inflation, seizure, systemic collapse, legal overreach, mobility loss?

What assets must remain functional in each scenario?

Which layers of control do I own outright, and which do I outsource?

Who knows what I own? And what laws might compel them to disclose or restrict it?

Only once these questions are addressed can structure emerge.

The Core Pillars of a Silent Vault

A well-constructed Silent Vault rests on five interdependent pillars. Each represents a design principle, not a product. Your implementation will depend on capital, citizenships, values, and strategic foresight.

1. **Privacy Without Isolation**

A Silent Vault is *private*, but not *invisible*. The goal is to reduce your asset's *attack surface* without entering a paranoid or illegal domain. This may mean utilising structures like offshore LLCs, privacy-preserving digital assets, or decentralised storage solutions. It also means minimising unnecessary disclosures. *Every institution, advisor, or platform with knowledge of your holdings is a potential vector for exposure*—not necessarily malicious, but systemically vulnerable.

2. **Jurisdictional Arbitrage**

No single country can offer both freedom and predictability forever. The Silent Vault requires diversification across legal systems, not just markets. This might involve storing metals in Singapore while holding crypto in self-custody in Estonia, and maintaining secondary banking access in Liechtenstein. A bank account in your home country is not a vault. It's a user interface to your regulator's whim.

3. **Redundant Access Channels**

You must assume that some systems will break—technically, legally, or politically. The Silent Vault must contain *at least one asset class that functions without third-party permission*, and ideally one that can be liquidated across borders in a compressed time window. This is not doomsday prep. It is operational realism.

4. **Liquidity Layering**

Wealth that cannot move is not protection—it's theatre. Your vault must contain *layers* of liquidity: fast-access assets for emergencies, intermediate assets for economic volatility, and hard-to-touch anchors for long-term preservation. Think in gradients: from instant (e.g. decentralised stablecoins) to delayed (e.g. offshore trusts or equity positions with lock-ups).

5. **Discretion-by-Design**

A vault's power is in *not needing to be used* until required. That means building systems that do not signal wealth to peers, authorities, or platforms. It also means separating identity from ownership where appropriate—through legal wrappers, multi-signature arrangements, or distributed storage. This is not about hiding; it is about *decoupling identity from vulnerability*.

Case Application: The Modular Vault in Action

Let us consider the hypothetical case of Maria, a German entrepreneur who holds €2.5 million across various assets. She is not wealthy enough to disappear behind institutional walls, but too capitalised to trust surface-level protections.

Her Silent Vault blueprint includes:

€150,000 in decentralised stablecoins across three wallets, with private keys stored using a multi-signature configuration involving two relatives in different countries.

A Singaporean safety deposit box with a mixture of gold and hard currency, accessed via a trustee with pre-signed authorisation in case of travel bans.

Equity stakes in private companies held through a Nevis LLC with German tax compliance managed by an offshore-aware accountant.

A self-directed pension fund partially invested in geographically uncorrelated assets, including farmland in Uruguay.

A digital backup of important documents, estate instructions, and legal powers of attorney encrypted and stored in multiple decentralised cloud platforms.

Each layer performs a function: resilience, discretion, access, and time-sensitive deployment. Together, they form a *non-obvious architecture*. No single pillar is invincible, but the *system's totality is asymmetrically robust.*

Building Your Blueprint: A Stepwise Mental Model

To avoid reactive or fragmented action, use the following mental model to begin shaping your own vault:

1. **Scenario Anchoring** – Define your critical risks. Inflation? Currency collapse? Legal overreach? Family dependency? Map your future assumptions without sugar-coating.

2. **Control Mapping** – Audit your current asset locations, custodians, legal exposure, and mobility. Who has to say "yes" for you to use what you own?

3. **Access Stress Test** – Practise accessing key assets under simulated constraints: 24-hour flight notice, internet outage, domestic capital lockup. Where does your plan crack?

4. **Layered Response Plan** – Design for different time horizons: 24 hours, 30 days, 5 years. Each horizon requires different assets, structures, and legal clarity.

5. **Legacy Integration** – Your vault must outlast you. Document intent, inheritance protocols, and operational instructions. Sovereignty is incomplete if it dies with you.

Counterpoints: The Moral Question of Building Silently

It is worth acknowledging the critique: is asset protection inherently antisocial? Does the Silent Vault represent withdrawal, or responsible foresight? There is no single answer, but there is clarity in asking:

Are you protecting wealth from legitimate tax or unjust seizure?

Are you defending capital for vanity or responsibility?

Are your assets structured to disappear—or to endure?

The vault is only as ethical as its architect. A well-built Silent Vault *can enable generosity, intergenerational resilience, and principled independence.* It is not inherently selfish. But it is *inherently strategic.*

Final Design Principles: Quiet, Clear, and Intentional

A successful Silent Vault does not look like a fortress. It looks like *nothing at all.* It is invisible to those who would misuse knowledge, resilient under duress, and elegant in its modularity.

Three principles guide its construction:

Silence – No centralisation, no signalling, no fragility.

Structure – Every asset is placed for a reason, in a jurisdiction by choice, and under a wrapper that respects your ethical and legal boundaries.

Sovereignty – At every decision point, ask: *If denied access, can I still act? If asked to justify, am I compliant? If I vanish, can my loved ones continue?*

The blueprint is not finished in a weekend. Nor should it be. It is a lifelong pattern of refinement. It changes as laws change, as values evolve, as new tools emerge.

But the intent is always the same: *build not just to survive—but to endure without asking for permission.*

Conclusion
The Sovereign Mind in a Dependent World

If you've arrived at this point, it's no longer mere curiosity carrying you forward. You're here because something in these pages struck a chord—because you've begun to see the world differently, perhaps even irreversibly so.

You've sensed it: the bedrock institutions once believed to be solid—banks, borders, rule of law, state-issued currencies—are not what they seemed. They are not immovable. They are, more often than not, contingent constructs, subject to revision without notice and often without your consent. And so you read on—not out of fascination, but out of a deeper resolve. A conviction, perhaps, that safeguarding your wealth isn't about avarice, but autonomy. That waiting for the old normal to return isn't caution—it's complacency masquerading as hope.

This isn't a recap. What follows doesn't summarise. Instead, this final chapter returns to the soul of what's been unfolding beneath the surface—a quieter, more private reckoning: the metamorphosis from passive participant to responsible steward. From being a citizen of convenience to becoming, in a very real sense, the custodian of your own sovereignty. The aim of this book was never just to show you how to construct a "vault." Its purpose was to alter your sense of what's truly worth locking away—and who should be entrusted with the key.

Let's speak plainly. This isn't only about finances. It never was. Asset protection is, at heart, a struggle over agency. It raises a fundamental question: who decides the terms of your life? In every era, every jurisdiction, every upheaval, that question re-emerges, often when you least expect it. The vault, in this light, is not simply a financial tool—it's a quiet refusal. A statement that says, without fanfare, I do not answer to your ledger, your embargo, or your interpretation of risk.

What we're grappling with, when we strip away the abstractions, is a kind of existential bookkeeping. And not just economic. It spans the psychological, the legal, the moral. Every choice you make about where your capital lives, what form it takes, and which laws it obeys—that's a reflection of your private theory of power. Not ideological power, but actual, hands-on authority: who can grant you access, who can deny your exit, and who inherits what you've built when you're gone.

Which brings us here. To the final hinge point—not a conclusion, but a quiet call to act. This chapter doesn't offer closure; it issues a challenge. It doesn't ask for agreement. It asks for authorship. The materials are on the table. The blueprints have been drafted. Now the question shifts: What will you create with them? And what inner posture will guide your construction?

You don't need all the answers today. But you do need to decide who gets to ask the questions.

The Illusion of Safety vs. the Architecture of Resilience

Most people, even many professionals, confuse *safety* with *lack of disruption.* If their assets are accessible, their accounts unflagged, their taxes processed without friction—they assume the system is working in their favour. But this is a misreading. *Safety is not the absence of trouble; it is the capacity to function when trouble arrives.*

You do not need to believe in collapse to prepare for dislocation. History is not shaped by averages. It is shaped by shocks—by sudden legal reversals, freezes on capital outflows, algorithmic account closures, or politicised scrutiny masquerading as compliance.

If there is one idea worth engraving into your operational mindset, it is this: *Resilience must be structural, not situational.* You cannot negotiate freedom while under duress. You must design for it *before* you need it.

What You've Actually Built

By now, your blueprint is no longer theoretical. You have thought in layers—across jurisdictions, across timelines, across custodial models. You've explored the ethical tensions of sovereignty. You've redefined liquidity not just as access to cash, but as access to *action.* You've reframed real estate, citizenship, and digital presence as tools of either entrapment or autonomy.

What you now hold is not just a vault of assets, but a *philosophical architecture.* One that operates in the background of your life—quiet, legal, deliberate. One that minimises the need to react because it was built to adapt.

You have moved from visibility to discretion, from fragility to redundancy, from centralisation to modular control. And you've done so not to escape the world, but to engage with it on your own terms.

Sovereignty Is Not a Personality Type. It's a System Design.

Some critics will argue that this kind of planning is antisocial—that it signals a lack of trust, a flight from civic responsibility, or even a form of paranoia. But this critique misunderstands the project entirely.

You are not opting out of society. You are *refusing dependency on systems that refuse accountability.*

You are not hoarding wealth. You are *stewarding resources across time, jurisdictions, and generations.*

You are not avoiding taxation or law. You are *choosing jurisdictions where law is consistent, and taxation is transparent and proportional.*

Sovereignty is not about building walls. It is about *building bridges you can control the access to.*

This distinction matters. Because as the line between compliance and coercion blurs, *your ability to design systems that honour your ethics while defending your autonomy becomes not just a technical skill—but a civic necessity.*

The Real Endgame: Psychological Ownership

We often speak of asset protection as if it's about numbers, documents, or vaults. But those are only proxies for something deeper: *the felt sense that your life's work is not subject to arbitrary revocation.*

True protection is the opposite of anxiety. It is clarity. It is the confidence that you can act under pressure without begging permission. It is the absence of behavioural distortion caused by fear of confiscation, surveillance, or sudden financial immobility.

This is not achieved by owning "safe" assets alone. It is achieved by owning assets in *safe systems*—where "safe" does not mean free from risk, but *aligned with your intent.*

This is the difference between control and ownership. The illusion of wealth is: "I have it, so I control it." The reality, especially in regulated digital economies, is often the reverse: "I am allowed to access it—so long as I behave predictably."

So What Happens Next?

This book does not end with a checklist. It ends with a question: *What system will you build, quietly, legally, and intentionally, that allows your wealth to serve your life—not vice versa?*

You do not need to be a lawyer or programmer. You need to be the architect of your own structure. You need to know what is non-negotiable, what must remain portable, and what you are unwilling to delegate to bureaucracy, convenience, or ideological drift.

If the sovereign individual is a myth, it is only because *so few take the time to construct themselves as one.* You now have the tools. The question is no longer what is possible. The question is what you will prioritise.

Your Silent Vault is not a product. It is a practice. Not a reaction to fear, but a statement of clarity. A decision to be the custodian—not just of capital, but of *capacity*.

Because when the systems fail, or glitch, or threaten you with their version of security, *you will already have yours*—quietly, fully, and on your terms.

The Freedom No One Can Revoke

Reminding readers that the truest wealth is the freedom to choose

Freedom is not an abstraction. It is not a philosophical motif, a rhetorical flourish, or the subject of a university debate. Freedom—real, operational freedom—is the *capacity to choose and act without asking for permission*. It is measured not in flags or slogans, but in your ability to relocate your capital, rewrite your contracts, reshape your environment, or walk away from systems that no longer serve you. And in a world where laws change faster than financial planning horizons, *that capacity is the rarest—and most defensible—form of wealth*.

If there is a single principle that anchors this book, it is this: *Freedom is the only asset that cannot be seized, devalued, or revoked by decree—if it is structured correctly*. That form of structuring is neither ideological nor utopian. It is legal. It is technical. It is psychological. And it begins with recognising that most people do not lose their freedom all at once—they *leak* it slowly, transaction by transaction, default by default, until all that remains is optionality in name only.

This subchapter is not a motivational coda. It is a call to precision. Because if freedom is the ultimate asset, it must be treated like one: protected, allocated, diversified, and insulated from counterparties who do not have your interests at heart.

Let us make that concrete.

Choice Is a Scarce Commodity in a Permissioned World

The modern world runs on permissions. Passports grant permission to move. Banks grant permission to spend. Governments grant permission to own, build, and even speak in certain contexts. This infrastructure of permission is often mistaken for security—but it is more accurately described as *conditional access*. Your privileges, no matter how enshrined in law or backed by tradition, can be suspended, frozen, flagged, or reinterpreted at the stroke of a bureaucratic pen or the shift of a geopolitical wind.

The reality is stark: *If your access to your own assets depends on continued alignment with systems that do not tolerate dissent, you do not own those assets. You rent them.*

Consider the high-profile cases of politically exposed persons in both the West and East whose accounts were frozen not due to fraud, but narrative deviation. Or take the average citizen in a fragile democracy whose pension fund, denominated in local currency, is effectively worth less with every week of inflation. These are not edge cases. These are warning signs of a system built on revocable participation.

Contrast this with the individual who holds digital assets in self-custody, with exit options across multiple jurisdictions, and with the practical means to move, transact, and rebuild without starting from zero. That is not theory. That is *design*. That is *structural freedom*.

The True Meaning of "Asset Protection" Is Option Preservation

To protect assets is not merely to shield them from loss. It is to *ensure that they can still generate choices when it matters most*. The core value of having a silent vault, a second passport, a portable portfolio, or a decentralised income stream is not the raw balance on a ledger—it is the *uninterrupted continuity of choice*.

The individual who can choose where to live, how to work, what to say, and when to exit is wealthier—strategically, psychologically, and ethically—than the millionaire who cannot transfer $10,000 abroad without triggering a compliance inquiry.

Freedom, then, is not just a lifestyle ideal. It is a *governance structure for your life.* And like all systems of governance, it must be audited, updated, and periodically tested under pressure.

Freedom Without Structure Is Fragile. Structure Without Freedom Is Tyranny.

There are two main errors people make when trying to secure their lives. The first is *failing to build systems at all*—assuming that their freedoms are permanent because they have existed in the past. The second is *overcorrecting into rigidity*—creating paranoid, inflexible setups that mistake fear for resilience.

Both are mistakes. True sovereignty is not rigidity. It is *liquidity of action embedded in structure.* That means legal clarity without overexposure. Custodial redundancy without unnecessary complexity. Psychological readiness without chronic anxiety.

As the Stoics understood, it is not enough to be free in theory. You must be free in *function.* That requires engineering your life in a way that makes escape a feature, not a failure. Where adaptation is not a trauma response but a built-in capacity.

In that sense, this is not about opting out of systems. It is about *becoming immune to their dysfunction.*

The Paradox of Preparation: You Hope Not to Need It—Until You Do

One of the most difficult truths to absorb is that the freer you are, the less your life should visibly change when systems falter. The work of preparation, if done correctly, results in a kind of *quiet normalcy* when others are scrambling.

This is not always easy to reconcile with the social impulse to stay visibly aligned with the status quo. To prepare silently, to hold options your peers do not, to walk away from volatility while others are trapped within it—these are not simply strategic acts. They are psychological decisions that require inner permission to *be different.*

Because freedom is lonely. Not ideologically, but *structurally.* When you no longer rely on a singular employer, a singular jurisdiction, a singular currency, or a singular platform—you will find yourself in a new category of human: one who has optionality, but must *choose what to care about with clarity.*

That is why *freedom must be paired with purpose.* Not just what you can walk away from, but what you are walking toward.

Legacy Is Not What You Leave Behind—It's What You Build While Still Able to Choose

Asset protection is often framed in defensive terms. But its highest form is generative. It creates space. Space for thinking, building, relocating, teaching, transmitting. A sovereign life is not only one that avoids dependence. It is one that *enables creation without permission.*

That may mean helping a family member start fresh in a new country. It may mean funding a project outside the bounds of legacy finance. It may mean simply maintaining the psychological freedom to think independently in a system designed to incentivise conformity.

Freedom is not selfish. It is foundational. And when wielded with clarity, it becomes not only a shield, but a gift.

The Litmus Test of Wealth: Could You Still Act If Everything Changed Tomorrow?

Forget portfolio size. Forget asset class. Ask instead:

If your bank account was frozen tomorrow, could you continue operating?

If your government shifted overnight, would you still have legal pathways to safety?

If the rules of the platform changed, could you re-establish your life without public appeal or media sympathy?

These are not paranoid questions. They are *design questions.* And the person who has answered them—and built accordingly—*already owns a freedom no one can revoke.*

Because when the systems around you destabilise, your capacity to act—legally, quickly, without begging—*is the final measure of wealth.*

The Freedom to Choose Is Not Given. It Is Constructed.

The enduring myth of modern liberalism is that freedom is the natural state of the individual—that it is guaranteed by virtue of citizenship, nationality, or social contract. This is a dangerous illusion. *Freedom is not given. It is built, maintained, and occasionally defended.*

The materials are not esoteric: jurisdictional awareness, legal redundancy, platform independence, psychological clarity. But the blueprint is not printed in public. It must be assembled by the individual.

You have now seen every piece. The only question that remains is: *Will you build a life in which your freedom is permanent, portable, and private?*

Because in the final audit, the only wealth worth counting is *your ability to act when it matters most*—without asking for permission, and without waiting for normal to return.

That is the freedom no one can revoke.

About the Author

Adrian Vossari is a global strategist, economic historian, and independent wealth resilience advisor known for his uncompromising approach to financial sovereignty in unstable times. With a background that spans geopolitical finance, alternative currencies, and underground asset networks, he's spent the last two decades helping individuals, families, and entrepreneurs fortify their wealth against systemic failure. Vossari's work fuses ancient strategies with modern tools—from barter economies to blockchain, from offshore havens to digital fortresses—empowering readers to not just protect their assets but reclaim their autonomy. He has lived across five continents, observed multiple economic collapses up close, and believes that true wealth is not just measured in digits—but in freedom.

www.ingramcontent.com/pod-product-compliance
Lightning Source LLC
Chambersburg PA
CBHW031340230926
51848CB00002B/325
* 9 7 8 9 3 7 1 3 4 1 7 8 3 *